T0317618

Business Transformation

Wiley & SAS Business Series

The Wiley & SAS Business Series presents books that help senior-level managers with their critical management decisions.

Titles in the Wiley & SAS Business Series include:

Activity-Based Management for Financial Institutions: Driving Bottom-Line Results by Brent Bahnub

Bank Fraud: Using Technology to Combat Losses by Revathi Subramanian

Big Data Analytics: Turning Big Data into Big Money by Frank Ohlhorst

Branded! How Retailers Engage Consumers with Social Media and Mobility by Bernie Brennan and Lori Schafer

Business Analytics for Customer Intelligence by Gert Laursen

Business Analytics for Managers: Taking Business Intelligence beyond Reporting by Gert Laursen and Jesper Thorlund

The Business Forecasting Deal: Exposing Bad Practices and Providing Practical Solutions by Michael Gilliland

Business Intelligence Applied: Implementing an Effective Information and Communications Technology Infrastructure by Michael Gendron

Business Intelligence in the Cloud: Strategic Implementation Guide by Michael S. Gendron

Business Intelligence Success Factors: Tools for Aligning Your Business in the Global Economy by Olivia Parr Rud

CIO Best Practices: Enabling Strategic Value with Information Technology, Second Edition by Joe Stenzel

Connecting Organizational Silos: Taking Knowledge Flow Management to the Next Level with Social Media by Frank Leistner

Credit Risk Assessment: The New Lending System for Borrowers, Lenders, and Investors by Clark Abrahams and Mingyuan Zhang

Credit Risk Scorecards: Developing and Implementing Intelligent Credit Scoring by Naeem Siddiqi

The Data Asset: How Smart Companies Govern Their Data for Business Success by Tony Fisher

Delivering Business Analytics: Practical Guidelines for Best Practice by Evan Stubbs

Demand-Driven Forecasting: A Structured Approach to Forecasting, Second Edition by Charles Chase

Demand-Driven Inventory Optimization and Replenishment: Creating a More Efficient Supply Chain by Robert A. Davis

The Executive's Guide to Enterprise Social Media Strategy: How Social Networks Are Radically Transforming Your Business by David Thomas and Mike Barlow

Economic and Business Forecasting: Analyzing and Interpreting Econometric Results by John Silvia, Azhar Iqbal, Kaylyn Swankoski, Sarah Watt, and Sam Bullard

Executive's Guide to Solvency II by David Buckham, Jason Wahl, and Stuart Rose

Fair Lending Compliance: Intelligence and Implications for Credit Risk Management by Clark R. Abrahams and Mingyuan Zhang

Foreign Currency Financial Reporting from Euros to Yen to Yuan: A Guide to Fundamental Concepts and Practical Applications by Robert Rowan

Health Analytics: Gaining the Insights to Transform Health Care by Jason Burke

Heuristics in Analytics: A Practical Perspective of What Influences Our Analytical World by Carlos Andre Reis Pinheiro and Fiona McNeill

Human Capital Analytics: How to Harness the Potential of Your Organization's Greatest Asset by Gene Pease, Boyce Byerly, and Jac Fitz-enz

Implement, Improve and Expand Your Statewide Longitudinal Data System: Creating a Culture of Data in Education by Jamie McQuiggan and Armistead Sapp

For more information on any of the above titles, please visit www.wiley.com.

Business Transformation

A Roadmap for Maximizing
Organizational Insights

Aiman Zeid

WILEY

Published by John Wiley & Sons, Inc., Hoboken, New Jersey.
Published simultaneously in Canada.

For general information on our other products and services or for technical support, please contact our Customer Care Department within the United States at (800) 762-2974, outside the United States at (317) 572-3993 or fax (317) 572-4002.

Wiley publishes in a variety of print and electronic formats and by print-on-demand. Some material included with standard print versions of this book may not be included in e-books or in print-on-demand. If this book refers to media such as a CD or DVD that is not included in the version you purchased, you may download this material at http://booksupport.wiley.com. For more information about Wiley products, visit www.wiley.com.

Library of Congress Cataloging-in-Publication Data

Zeid, Aiman.
    Business transformation : a roadmap for maximizing organizational insights / Aiman Zeid.
        pages   cm. — (Wiley & SAS business series)
    Includes index.
    ISBN 978-1-118-72465-1 (hardback); ISBN 978-1-118-89148-3 (ebk);
ISBN 978-1-118-89161-2 (ebk)
        1. Information technology—Management.   2. Organizational behavior.
    3. Organizational change.   4. Business planning.   I. Title.
    HD30.2.Z444   2014
    658.4'038—dc 3
                                                                    2013047059

10 9 8 7 6 5 4 3 2 1

Contents

Foreword

When *Information Revolution*[1] was published in 2006, no Chinese-based companies were among the top 10 largest companies by market capitalization. Apple didn't sell phones. Facebook was something college kids used to connect with their friends. Back then, we talked a lot about the amount of data coming in and faster processing speed.

What we believed then remains true today: Data, and the decision-making process, can be moved throughout the organization to equip every decision maker (automated, line worker, analyst, executive) to make the best choices. By operationalizing analytics, organizations can identify and quantify both opportunity and risk. *Information Revolution* highlighted SAS' Information Evolution Model, which helps organizations understand how they interact with their information and how to extract more value from it through analytics.

SO WHAT HAS CHANGED?

Business intelligence still matters. But today's global economy requires predictive analytics and forecasting to play a more active role. Insights from unstructured data now hold great promise. New ways to store, move, and process data have made big data more accessible and affordable than ever before. Delivery has moved to mobile. Many leaders run their businesses from tablets and smartphones.

A persistent myth is that technology alone enables all this. Sure, you need technology, but it's just one component: People, information processes, and culture are equally critical. That's really what this book is about—transforming your organization to harness all four components.

PUTTING THE SPOTLIGHT ON PEOPLE AND CULTURE

After *Information Revolution* was published, accelerated processing speeds gave rise to near-real-time results. More granular exploration of data became possible in ways that weren't quick or easy before. Organizations that treat their data as an asset continue to:

> Invest in people with the skills to extract the insights that were hidden in the data and surface them to decision makers throughout the organizations.

> Foster a culture that encourages using data to uncover new business opportunities and gain a better understanding of their customers.

> Have an executive sponsor who leads the effort to find, hire, cultivate, and support individuals who embrace fact-based decision making. This executive sponsor pays particular attention to the communication challenge that data-driven decision making presents. It's important to have an executive who can articulate what the analytical insight returns can mean to the business units—and win over skeptics.

If top executives still make decisions based on gut feeling and data-driven individuals are still a separate part of the business, no amount of technology and data governance processes will make a difference. But if an organization is committed to using data successfully, one strategic hire can have a huge impact. A new type of professional, the data scientist, can bridge the communication gap that prevents an analytical culture from taking hold. Tom Davenport, in his *Harvard Business Review* article "Data Scientist: The Sexiest Job of the 21st Century,"[2] describes a data scientist this way: "It's a high-ranking professional with the training and curiosity to make discoveries in the world of big data. . . . Their sudden appearance on the business scene reflects the fact that organizations are now wrestling with information that comes in varieties and volumes never encountered before." Data scientists help organizations get the most out of their data, in part, by using business requirements to drive the information exploration and the application of analytics. Data scientists often have a background in math, statistics, and computer science, but aren't necessarily experts in any one of those fields. They have to be very good at translating the value of data to the business and helping analysts understand what they need to do.

Internal communication and business and IT alignment continue to present challenges for organizations. Many rely on enterprise Centers of Excellence to boost business-transformation efforts.

My point is: You can't just bring in technology tools to solve your business problems and expect them to do all the work. You must have the infrastructure capabilities, the skilled people, the information processes, and the cultural commitment to derive the most value from your data.

AND SOME THINGS STAY THE SAME . . .

Some things haven't changed, and one of them is taking a structured approach to building toward the enterprise level of information maturity—and beyond. The five levels outlined in 2006 remain relevant today (though we've grouped the levels into three key categories). Unfortunately, many organizations are in a quandary about how to reach information maturity. Now here's the clincher: "By 2015, 15 percent of organizations will modernize their strategy for information management capability and exhibit a 20 percent higher financial performance than their peers," according to Gartner.[3] These are clear signs of strategic initiatives by many organizations to reach higher maturity level.

To get started, you need to understand where your organization is today before you can build toward the future. This is particularly important as it relates to purchasing technology. Organizations that say they have not received a strong return on their investment in analytic technology frequently suffer from information maturity issues and may benefit from a business-transformation effort. Assessing maturity is a process, but well worth the effort in the knowledge you will gain. It can be painful to find out your organization is not at the maturity level you assumed. But, you will have a clear picture of how to begin developing your road map to get to the next level.

A fact-based decision-making culture is no longer an option; it's a requirement spreading across industries. To stay competitive, be proactive. Use the Information Evolution Model. Let your data give you a fresh perspective on your business—see what's working, fix what isn't, and set your sights on new opportunities.

—Jim Davis
Senior Vice President and
Chief Marketing Officer
SAS

NOTES

1. Jim Davis, Gloria J. Miller, and Allan Russell, *Information Revolution: Using the Information Evolution Model to Grow Your Business* (Hoboken, NJ: John Wiley & Sons, 2006).
2. Thomas H. Davenport and D. J. Patil, "Data Scientist: The Sexiest Job of the 21st Century," *Harvard Business Review*, October 2012, http://hbr.org/2012/10/data-scientist-the-sexiest-job-of-the-21st-century/ar/1.
3. Eric Thoo, Mark A. Beyer, Ted Friedman, Merv Adrian, and Andreas Bitterer, "Predicts 2013: Advancing Data Management Maturity," Gartner, December 10, 2012.

Preface

Over the past 28 years of my professional career, I had the opportunity and privilege to work with many clients in almost all industries and sectors in the United States, Europe, the Middle East, Asia, and Latin America. I have helped these clients improve their efficiency, change their operating models, and transform their organizations. Although each region has business and cultural differences, all organizations face the same types of core challenges when they look closely at their operating models and evaluate their efficiency and alignment. When organizations realize they have a weakness in their decision-making process, strategy, or business functions, the first impulse is go with the easy answer first. Often in my travels I've seen a new technology being touted as a cure-all. And while new technology might be needed, the business results could vary considerably. Visionary leaders and executives realize that the key to unlocking their organization's full potential requires honest and objective observation and evaluation of how the organization conducts its daily routine tasks.

Two key obvious ingredients are required to develop strategy and make sound decisions—information and skills. Accurate and consistent information provides a detailed understanding of business performance. People with the right skills can explore this information and analyze it to help their organization make sound decisions. This may be all organizations need if they limit their view to specific tasks or functions. But the focus should always be on enterprise performance. The formula for an efficient operating model will now need two more ingredients. Decision makers from various business units need to interact and collaborate to make the right decisions for the enterprise. Then the human nature characteristics and challenges quickly bring our attention to the internal organization culture that we all recognize in our individual environments. Each environment has its own unique formal and informal business practices, norms, and expectations that influence how decisions are made.

Aligning all business units around enterprise performance can be difficult. Effective organizational transformations can achieve alignment when organizations focus on their four key pillars—people, processes, technical infrastructure, and culture. The winning organizational transformation formula is now complete. When I visit clients I emphasize that it doesn't matter that you've mastered one, or even two, of these factors—you need to work on all of them to bring your organization into alignment and truly transform it. Think of it like a recipe. Cut out a key ingredient, or substitute a poor alternative, and the recipe won't taste the same—it might not even work. It's the same with organizational transformation. If you ignore the culture part, the best technical infrastructure in the world won't help you improve the organization's business performance.

Many visionary leaders and executives realize the need to take a comprehensive look at their organizations. Addressing weaknesses and leveraging strengths in the current capabilities in each environment requires business transformation efforts in many cases. Leaders who realize that and, more important, act quickly can produce significant results for their organizations. I wrote this book because many executives still struggle with how and where to start. Approaching these complex organizational challenges needs a structured approach and a sound strategy that is tailored for each environment. This has been a significant focus of my professional career, and I wanted to share my experience and provide a roadmap for organizations to follow.

Acknowledgments

Writing this book would not have been possible without the encouragement and support I received from my family and colleagues. Their support gave me the energy and inspiration I needed to make the time to write this book after long days in the office and many business trips. I dedicate this book to my wife Marianne for her patience, support, and tolerance of my work and travel schedule, and to my children Suzanne and Adam, of whom I am very proud. The support I received from my colleagues at SAS has been invaluable. I would like to especially thank Michi Johnson, Christina Harvey, Cathy Traugot, and Stacey Hamilton for the contributions and support they provided.

CHAPTER 1

The Critical Role of Business Insight

Have you ever asked a question that no one in your organization could answer? Or maybe someone answered it, but it turned out the information driving the answer was so flawed that you really got no answer at all. Or maybe you got multiple conflicting answers that took hours, days—or maybe even weeks to straighten out.

Have you ever wondered why—in an age when bar codes are on everything, every conversation with a customer is recorded, and the Internet is full of comments about your products and services—you don't really know who your customers are? Or what they want? Or, more important, what they might want next year? Are you frustrated because your organization isn't achieving its goals? Or are you wondering why your organization is not keeping up with the competition?

You are not alone. Information, and the business insight you can derive from it, is coming so fast, from so many sources, in so many different formats, and at such incredible volumes that it is difficult to grasp. It's not hyperbole to suggest that gaining insight from data is like drinking water from a fire hose. Business insight is derived from an organization's information by using the domain knowledge of its resources and applying analytics to mine the data for critical trends, forecast revenue, determine customer propensity to buy products and

1

services, and predict attrition in critical talent. Business insight is also produced by using business intelligence for querying and reporting, performance management to monitor critical business key performance indicators (KPIs) and validate strategies, and industry solutions to optimize the operations of critical business functions. Deriving business insight depends on developing an enterprise information foundation to properly integrate data from all business units in the organization. Organizations also have to take advantage of external and unstructured data to develop business insight. Yet most organizations find they can't generate the information they need (from their data)—or, if they can, it is not coming fast enough to make a difference.

Business insight adds value in several areas, ranging from a simple view of historical performance driven by the use of business intelligence to predictions of sales volumes and customer behaviors developed by the use of analytics. Successful organizations create a competitive advantage by maximizing the use of analytics to guide their decision making and strategies. This book highlights the importance of developing and aligning the organization's resources and talents, information infrastructure, and use of analytics with the required processes and culture to create business insights that strengthen its competitive advantage.

You have questions, your organization has data—but can you generate the insight you need from the data? And can you do it fast enough? You need more than technology, a team of consultants, or a visionary data guru to lead you out of the data forest. You need a comprehensive approach to evolve your current information management practices to generate more insight. You need to introduce new talent, new processes, and a new culture that will help make your organization more data-driven and analytical. You need to promote the use of analytics and insight across the organization in a repeatable and effective way, and learn how to identify a starting point and develop a strategy for getting this done. And that's what you will read about in this book.

THE DISRUPTIVE NATURE OF DATA

During the recent U.S. presidential election there was a spirited discussion around whether aggregating poll data could accurately predict its outcome. Much of the debate related to the work of a blogger and statistician named Nate Silver (www.fivethirtyeight.com). Silver built a model that weighs and averages numerous polls based on multiple factors. Every few days, on his blog, he would update the percentage chances that Mitt Romney and Barack Obama had of winning the election. In 2008, Silver's model of the presidential election was accurate to within one percentage point of the final popular vote,[1] and he correctly predicted the race in 49 of 50 states. But at that time he was a comparatively unknown blogger. In 2010, his blog was licensed to the *New York Times*, and in the fall of 2012 he had recently published a book.[2] As his 2012 model increasingly showed a likely victory for the incumbent (it stood at 90.9 percent the day of the election), pundits began to howl. Some tried to pick apart the model, while others claimed bias. But one savvy commentator noted what was really up: Silver was a disruptive force. "Silver's work poses a threat to more traditional—and, in particular, to more excitable—forms of political punditry and horse-race journalism,"[3] explained a *Washington Post* columnist. Silver was threatening a traditional profession. And it wasn't his first time. Silver initially gained notice for forecasting professional baseball player and team performance by using less traditional statistical measures. A variation on his system was adopted by the Oakland Athletics baseball team's general manager, who hired an analyst and began selecting players based on skills that weren't as highly valued in the marketplace. The book *Moneyball*,[4] by Michael Lewis, captured the tension fueled by the general manager's decision to ditch the conventional wisdom of scouts who looked at traditional statistics. Despite regular declarations that "moneyball" is "dead,"[5] it not only survives but also continues to grow as more teams, both inside and outside of baseball, hire analysts.

AN UNCONVENTIONAL LOOK AT CONVENTIONAL WISDOM

In the business world the corollary to the pundits and scouts are those buyers and marketing gurus—even CEOs—who operate on "gut" instinct in choosing what products to launch and what business path to follow. They are often rather hostile to the Nate Silvers, who invaded their territory with analysis that suggests a different path.

Unfortunately, businesses tend to have far too many pundits and not nearly enough Nate Silvers. So even if an organization purchases software or a solution to begin to drive the business more analytically, they don't have the people who can analyze the data, or work with the business unit to decide what to analyze. Or the organization doesn't have a culture in place that will accept the analysts' work, a process in place that makes analytics a factor in everyday decisions, and a leadership that understands that gut instinct is old school.

Conventional wisdom has a way of creeping into organizations and holding them hostage. Even companies whose executives talk about their "change management" are often entrenched in approaches and ways of doing business that aren't really working. An analytic project often provides the aha moment when an organization realizes everything it thought it knew—what its customers wanted, what was most likely to sell, what was its most profitable service—was not completely accurate. Let's explore a few of those moments.

Customer value is rife with examples. We all know our best customer, right? It's the one who buys the most stuff from us. Or is it? If you want to create an offer, or provide a discount, or do anything to increase the loyalty of your best customers you don't need analytics— you just need to know who spent the most money. Many telecommunication providers certainly worked under that assumption for years, until some of the savvier ones used insight from analytics to discover that their "best" customers were actually costing them a lot of money. These were the customers who tied up customer support with questions about their plan, subscribed to a plan that was not profitable, used the service in the least profitable way to the organization, or didn't keep up with their payments and had a high delinquency rate. All that attention to those high-needs customers was hurting the bottom line. Yet this flies in the face of conventional wisdom that suggests you do anything to keep a customer happy because it costs more to gain a new one than retain one.

Another example of the use of insight from information comes from the banking industry. Banks often have three critical functions operating in silos. The marketing department focuses on customer retention, product innovation, profitability, and the proper channels to promote them. The risk team develops and monitors operational risk factors and scores customers in terms of their liabilities and probability of default. The finance organization keeps its revenue and loss information in its own silo. Banks have operated these three critical functions in silos for years. When the information from these siloed functions is integrated, a brand new perspective provides more business insight for making better decisions and setting strategies. The actual revenue from each customer is produced from the financial side. The risk rating for each customer can be provided by the risk team, and now the marketing organization can use all it knows about the customers to identify the proper product to market to each one based on his or her risk score and total contribution to the bank's revenue. Banks can now develop a more effective strategy to grow their business with each of their customer segments based on insights derived from their information.

INNOVATING AT THE SPEED OF DATA

Both telecommunications and banking examples highlight the value of speed in working with data. It's one thing to figure out that certain customers aren't worth the effort to retain and decide not to send them an offer; it's another to do it in real time when a customer calls looking for a different rate plan or upgrade or walks into a branch to apply for a home mortgage. Does the service agent have a file that offers suggestions as to whether a discounted upgrade should be offered to the customer or whether a credit limit should be extended? Or should the agent just politely listen and ignore customers' threats to take their business elsewhere?

When organizations begin using analytical insight they challenge conventional wisdom quickly and effectively. An online floral company stopped gearing its advertising to men when it discovered most of the people buying flowers for various holidays were women. A casino directed its best discounts away from its most loyal customers (they were going to visit either way), and targeted them at the customers who were also visiting their competitors. Engineers on an oil rig use data on conditions in their environment to predict when equipment needs maintenance before a costly breakdown, rather than relying on the manufacturer's manual that had not proven effective in the past. Automobile companies predict which part may fail, and proactively replace it when a customer comes in for routine maintenance, saving money and increasing customer perception of quality. Hospitals use analytics to predict—at admission—which patients are at risk for readmission, and then plan treatment and discharge to keep them from being readmitted.

The value of insight goes beyond the business world in ways that a businessperson can certainly relate to. If you have a child getting ready to attend college or a university you have heard time and time again that their grades and their entrance exam scores will determine how well they will do. One college discovered that grades and entrance exams weren't the determining factor at all—it was when the students signed up for classes. Those signing up late were more likely to fail or drop out.

Even when the "gut" is backed up by data, analytics helps organizations blend in other data that puts these statistics into a different context. One insurer bucked conventional wisdom by scaling back its rate increases for families insuring teenage drivers. The 17-year-olds it insured didn't suddenly lose their propensity for fender benders and speeding tickets. Instead, the insurer discovered that over the lifetime of the family (both teens and parents), increasing the rates to cover expected claims actually drove some very loyal customers away permanently—and that was more costly for the company than covering the price of a new fender.

WEIGHING RISK AND BRINGING THE BETTER PART OF GUT INSTINCT BACK INTO THE EQUATION

The insurance example drives to the heart of what analytics and the business insight it generates is about, and what it isn't meant to do. Analytics doesn't replace innovation, it helps innovation flourish. By using insight to challenge conventional wisdom and weigh the success of new approaches, organizations can feel more confident about their choices. Short of cloning the DNA of Apple founder Steve Jobs, most organizations will succeed not on the cult appeal of an innovative leader, but on the success of many decisions made by many individuals *working with sound data*. If you are reading this book and consider yourself an innovator, think of analytics as your behind-the-scenes assistant that helps you test your bold ideas and gives a view of what the likely outcomes of your initiatives, products, and strategies may be in the future.

Analytics lets you put the gut instinct back into the discussion in a way that controls the downside. A simple example is the A/B testing in web marketing (where some visitors see the "A" page with certain recommendations and others see the "B" page with different recommendations). Test that novel idea, that catchy slogan, that interesting promotion—but do so in a controlled environment in which you can quickly, efficiently, and effectively analyze the outcome without dependence on time-consuming sampling. In a faster processing environment, you can test more granularly and run as many scenarios as you need.

There are more serious examples where innovation ran rampant without the steadying influence of business insight. The economic meltdown of the last decade certainly put a spotlight on some very innovative practices: no-doc mortgages, credit default swaps, and lots of chopping and repackaging of thinly secured debt. If the layers of oversight weren't steep enough prior to the meltdown, they're getting steeper today. Managing risk is the yin to innovation's yang. You want to manage risk without stifling innovation and without feeling beholden to the bean counters and frightened of the regulators. This is an area where analytics really shines. Use fast processing and you can manage risk more dynamically—in a way that actually drives innovation. New innovative high-performance analytics solutions are now contributing significant value to organizations in areas like risk, fraud, and others.

Credit card issuers illustrate the risk-to-innovation phenomenon in their efforts to make the proverbial lemonade from the sour stench of stolen credit cards. Forrester "estimates that globally merchants are paying between $200 billion and $250 billion in fraud losses annually, while banks and financial services organizations are losing between $12 billion and $15 billion annually."[6]

In a perfect world, issuers could stop the fraud before it happens. Easier said than done, as anyone knows who ever took that dream trip overseas without calling their credit card issuer first. The anger, frustration, fear, *embarrassment* of having a legitimate charge denied doesn't go a long way in developing a loyal lifetime customer. Pressed between losing money or losing a customer, issuers have tried to find better ways to target fraud without angering customers. Some of these efforts worked, but not in a timely way. Who hasn't gotten a call from a credit card company asking you if you recently purchased a television at a store you've never set foot in? Or through an online website you've never heard of?

But if you apply high-performance analytics, in a fast processing environment, to big data and create models that can predict fraudulent claims during the five-second window between when the sale is recorded and the bill is paid—now that's managing risk innovatively.

Note that the example added at least one phrase we haven't spent much time talking about: fast processing. Since *Information Revolution*[7] was published, there has been a real technical revolution in processing speed at modest cost. Today's cost factor for increased processing speed should not blow up the IT budget.

The speed is there. The data is there. The cost is reasonable. What is often lacking is the analytic know-how and the cultural structure. The linchpin of the card issuer's ability to decline a charge without irritating its customer is the skill to build a model that accurately understands whether the person who owns the card is buying the television (or someone else is), the data to run the model against, and the processing speed to do it in five seconds. An organization can't simply buy a solution that will let them determine with customer-pleasing accuracy (and then stop) a fraudulent credit card transaction in the five-second window between the time the card is swiped and the sale is finalized. It can buy a solution that might temporarily stop fraud without ticking off customers—until the fraudsters find a way around it. It might buy a solution that gets it right enough of the time so that it won't chase away too many customers. But technology alone will not consistently stop fraud or please customers.

For that you need the other organizational foundations to support analytics: people, processes, and culture.

PEOPLE, PROCESS, TECHNOLOGY, AND CULTURE

The first thing a credit card issuer that is successfully combating fraud must do is have a process in place for managing the data it will use to build a model that can tell the difference, in five seconds, between a legitimate and a fraudulent charge. *Data governance* is a term that doesn't get covered in the mainstream business press or discussed at executive board meetings. If the issuer doesn't know, for instance, that a customer on a spending binge at the local home improvement store just acquired a home mortgage from the organization's mortgage branch, the purchase of a riding lawn mower looks a little suspicious. The organization needs people who can drive this process, choosing the right data and using it in a disciplined fashion. Typically, these individuals have both business and technical knowledge and an affinity for talking to both sides of the "house." They are creative enough to use analytics to know what data (a new mortgage, credit scores, deposit movements) really matter—and which don't matter at all. And they understand how to create a consistent, replicable process that works over and over and over. If business units have the bureaucratic equivalent of armed guards patrolling outside their own information silos, and IT is rolling its eyes over the business case for analytics, then the organization will get stuck.

If you've picked up this book, you already have some general sense that analytics and business insight are something you need more of. You probably also reached the conclusion that a comprehensive business and organizational transformation is needed to generate this insight and, more important, convince the business consumers to use this insight to make decisions and validate strategies. Or you want to understand how you can expand on the business intelligence efforts that have served you well. You might have read about predictive analytics, forecasting, or high-performance analytics and you want to know how your organization can transform itself to get more deeply engaged in those processes. You might also be trying really hard to gain insight from analytics and be unable to figure out why it isn't working.

Or you might think you've got this all figured out and you're looking for validation.

Chances are your organization doesn't have it all figured out. Many organizations haven't achieved a level of maturity where the business units have called off the armed guards surrounding the information silos and the organization is taking an enterprise-wide view of the business. Instead, most organizations have multiple ad hoc and individual analytics efforts attempting to generate insight. This approach is not very effective, is not replicable, and can result in a lot of redundancies (with their attendant costs). A well-planned business and organizational transformation is needed to make the proper changes to move from the ad-hoc approach to a more repeatable process to use analytics to derive business insight.

For organizations struggling to get started and for those that feel they need to improve, this book outlines how to approach the development of a business and organizational transformation effort. This process is an endeavor to improve organization maturity and must be guided by a structured methodology.

This book uses the Information Evolution Model, a maturity model patented by SAS,[8] to help you develop your business transformation roadmap. Figure 1.1 illustrates the five levels of information and analytical maturity that can help you assess your organization's current capabilities. Knowing where you are sets the starting point of your journey. The model will also guide you in determining where you need to go and how to get there. A special emphasis is placed on the need to reach the Enterprise level so that organizations can focus on a holistic view of their operation and understand their value chain. The book also provides guidance in identifying a starting point for focusing your initial effort and launching your organization's business transformation. This leads to a discussion of how organizations can develop a strategy for their business transformation and a roadmap to implement their strategy objectives.

STARTING THE JOURNEY

If you've weathered the recent financial upheavals with minimal disruption, or are buffeted from competitive forces by brand leadership or monopoly, there is a tendency to view analytics and the value they deliver as something not worth the bother, especially if it involves changing a culture that is working just fine. The information in this book might seem like something that doesn't apply. Eventually, though, even market leaders are challenged, barriers to entry are lowered, natural monopolies disappear. Don't wait until that happens.

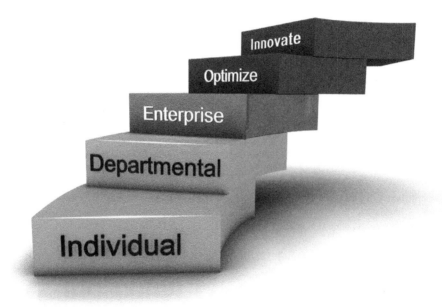

Figure 1.1   The Five Levels of the Information Evolution Model

When you reach the point at which you are reacting to pressure, it will be so much more expensive and time consuming to become a proactive, strategic organization.

When *Information Revolution* was published in 2006 the concept that maximizing the value of business insight required more than technology was a tough sell. The idea that people, processes, and culture were just as important—if not more so—was somewhat revolutionary. Since that time, more organizations have begun to share this vision and are engaged in determining their maturity, and you'll learn how they are progressing. By the time you finish reading this book you should have a better understanding of where your organization is at and how to reach the level that will allow the organization to use insight in a way that helps you thrive and grow.

Let's start that journey now.

NOTES

1. www.nytimes.com/2008/11/10/business/media/10silver.html?pagewanted=all.
2. Nate Silver, *The Signal and the Noise: Why So Many Predictions Fail—But Some Don't* (New York: Penguin, 2012).
3. www.washingtonpost.com/blogs/wonkblog/wp/2012/10/30/the-nate-silver-backlash/.
4. Michael Lewis, *Moneyball: The Art of Winning an Unfair Game* (New York: W.W. Norton, 2004).
5. http://mlb.sbnation.com/2012/10/26/3560434/moneyball-stats-scouts-brad-pitt-shirtless-come-on-google-traffic.
6. Andrew Cser, "The Forrester Wave: Enterprise Fraud Management, Q1 2013," Forrester Research Inc., February 13, 2013.
7. Jim Davis, Gloria J. Miller, and Allan Russell, *Information Revolution: Using the Information Evolution Model to Grow Your Business* (Hoboken, NJ: John Wiley & Sons, 2006).
8. D. A. Hatcher, W. M. Prentice, and R. A. Russell, "Enterprise Information Evolution Analysis System," U.S. Patent 7 752 070 B2, Assignee SAS Institute Inc., July 6, 2010.

CHAPTER **2**

The Journey: Taking the First Steps toward Transforming Your Organization

What we've learned so far: Business insights hold significant value for organizations in all industries and domains despite the fact that research suggests that 70 percent of organizations haven't achieved a level of maturity where appropriate business insight is developed and used effectively to drive decisions and validate strategies. So, the next question is, "Why?" Why are organizations not producing all the business insight they need or, even, why are they not producing sufficient insight to understand their customers' behavior and properly manage their risk using all the information they already have?

DIFFERENT APPROACHES

To answer the question of why this happens, let's think about the capabilities that exist in business units. When business units have a need to answer a business question, they typically use their business perspective and interpretation of their own performance to guide this process. They perform these tasks on a daily basis in any way they can to meet their deadlines. This may include using the IT team for some support. The same process is also completed when the organization as a whole has a need to produce, let's say, compliance reports to submit to regulators. The accuracy of these reports may not be the best an organization can produce. Furthermore, these processes are lengthy, especially if they require getting information from other business units. And, finally, these processes are inefficient. Many information management processes are duplicated over and over. The use of resources, especially analytical resources, is not optimized; neither is the use of business unit and IT infrastructure resources. All organizations are doing this today at various levels. And why wouldn't they? Business units must do something to get their work done, and using the resources they can control seems the most expeditious.

Does this sound familiar?

- A business issue becomes a priority because of a problem: a drop in sales or the erosion of profit. Everyone scrambles to react.
- A technical team is assembled.
- Data is gathered and analyzed.
- Information processes are repeated with different business perspectives leading to different interpretations and results.

Assuming the different interpretations can be resolved—and the project deemed a success—another problem emerges. Someone says, "Hey, let's do that again." But the technical team has moved on to put out another fire. So managers figure they need to expand those technical teams, or add more technical or analytical resources, and end up duplicating many tasks that are common to these ad hoc projects and requests.

This is a particular issue in model building and deployment, which is critical to successful predictive analytics approaches. It isn't enough to compute customer lifetime value once a year or once a quarter. Many companies talk about how they loved the results they got from those infrequent modeling runs, but they took too long to build or they took so long to run that tweaking them dragged the production cycle out. It becomes a project, rather than an ongoing process. One retailer had some terrific success automating markdowns (the process of picking the right price cut to help get the merchandise out the door). But over time the model broke down and was too cumbersome to rebuild. A well-defined and repeatable process was not used to extract and integrate the information.

With the growing demand to make decisions quickly, and to automate the results so that more business users can use them, these project-driven information management practices are not efficient. In addition, they don't produce accurate results when they require input from other business functions. Consequently, many decisions are made without information validations. And many organizations using these practices are not producing sufficient business insight to support their decisions.

A much better approach is for organizations to think of information as a corporate asset to be deliberately managed using a well-structured process. The process is managed with input from all stakeholders and with careful attention to minimizing duplication of efforts and maximizing the use of all resources (business, analytical, and technical). Get away from thinking about projects and instead think about an ongoing, flexible, holistic process that treats data—and what can be gleaned from it—as a strategic entity worthy of your time and attention.

JUGGLING MULTIPLE CHALLENGES

In addition to the challenges caused by their approach to information management, organizations are also facing issues involving both the information itself and the act of organizing it. Over the past five years there has been a significant increase in the amount of information gathered. New technologies make it much cheaper to store all this information, so every customer interaction is tracked and every product development step is monitored. Vast amounts of unstructured information are available through call center notes, warranty claims, social media, and more. Information is flowing in much faster than our current processes can handle.

In addition to the increase in data volume, there is also a visible increase in the complexity of the information available to us. Finally, government regulations and risk factors are always a concern. This new reality presents information management challenges. The IT team, dealing with these issues on a daily basis, focuses on cost control and an information architecture that can scale to handle the increased demand for processing power and information requests.

Organizations focus on the cost, and the management—but not on the organization. Every business unit is busy managing its own environment, and dare we say "silo" (more on that later), with too little attention paid to collaborating or sharing with other business units. Furthermore, individual business units use their own perspective to define how to interpret information and create business performance views. If marketing is measured on how many new customers it brings in, the description of a "new customer" might be different than in a sales unit where cross-marketing to existing customers is a key performance metric. So when an executive asks a seemingly simple question—"How many of our deposits are coming from new customers?"—multiple conflicting answers swarm in.

In addition, there is typically a limited supply of analytical and domain resources scattered around in business units—and no framework to use these skills efficiently across business units. Finally, there is the classic challenge in reaching a healthy and collaborative working relationship between business and IT. Why? Because business and IT have very different priorities and perspectives that can't be aligned without the intervention of an enterprise-level executive.

These organizational challenges are much harder to deal with than the information challenges, despite the fact that the information challenges tend to consume business unit and IT time. Dealing with both types of challenges is necessary, and the approach organizations choose to use can make a difference between producing actual results and continuing to deal with the symptoms.

For instance, when organizations realize they have a data quality problem, they may purchase software to clean their data. But fixing the information quality problem by cleaning *existing* data will not stop more dirty data from entering the organization's information environment. The organization needs to uncover the root cause of the poor quality data. Operational data entry processes may be one possible and obvious culprit. But a lack of consensus about how business units define or derive additional data elements such as profit, household, or customer segments may be the real culprit.

What organizations need to recognize is that these two very different types of challenges are interrelated and must be dealt with from an enterprise perspective simultaneously. If you suffer from asthma, you can keep running to the emergency room to get treated, or you can take preventive medicine to get at the underlying lung inflammation. Although not quite the same in information management and organization, you get the gist. Preventive medicine for the organization is a business transformation approach supported by the executive team. The approach should develop a common understanding of various competing priorities as well as build relationships between business units and between business and IT through well-established processes, consistent communication, and alignment of efforts. This book explores these organizational maturity qualities in later chapters.

HOW TO DEAL WITH CHALLENGES EFFECTIVELY

How do you deal with these challenges in a pragmatic and effective way? By transforming your organization's approach to information: to using it, managing it, organizing it, and—ultimately—analyzing it. The objective of business transformation efforts is to evolve the organization's maturity to a higher level. Increasing your organization's maturity requires focus on four key organizational pillars: people, processes, technical infrastructure, and culture (see Figure 2.1). And it is not something that can happen overnight. It is a journey.

The three key requirements to successfully embark on this journey are:

1. Securing continuous executive sponsorship

2. Understanding the current capabilities and dynamics of the four capability pillars

3. Aligning the capabilities of the four pillars with the organization's business objectives with the support of a Center of Excellence to develop the four pillars

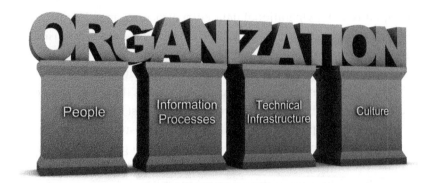

Figure 2.1 Organizational Capability Pillars

This book discusses many aspects of this journey. Let's start by exploring each of these key requirements in detail.

EXECUTIVE SPONSORSHIP: CRITICAL TO SUCCESS

Organizations genuinely interested in making long-lasting changes need a leader who can make them happen. Transforming an organization's approach to information affects the daily routine, the workforce, the information environment, the processes, and the operating model. It can upend the cultural paradigm. Executives need to support these efforts and give them visibility and priority. Visionary executives who believe in innovation understand the crucial role of information and analytics to transform their organizations into viable market competitors. Steve Jobs's consistent commitment to simplifying iPhone operations and using innovative new ways to communicate with users guided Apple to unprecedented success in the market. The success of Apple is an example of how a leader can develop and align the capabilities of an organization to not only achieve phenomenal financial performance levels, but to also reach a high level of market dominance.

Executive buy-in and meaningful involvement help organizations resolve conflicts and adjust course as they get their business initiatives off the ground. Executive support is also needed to monitor focus. Many organizations continue to focus on tactical work because this is the way they operated for years. When people are part of an organization with some operational history, it is sometimes hard for them to stop and ask themselves the question, "Is this work contributing to a critical organizational objective, or is it nice to have since we are so used to using the output of this task?" Business units sometimes struggle to shift to a more strategic approach. Executive sponsorship is critical to guiding business unit stakeholders and leaders to strike the right balance between tactical and strategic information management efforts.

UNDERSTANDING CURRENT CAPABILITIES

The second requirement speaks to the need to know what the organization has now, in order to understand what is needed to move forward. When we plan a trip or a project, we naturally have to define two key elements: The starting point and the destination or the final objectives. This organizational journey is no exception. Business transformation efforts focus on improving capabilities, skills, and the operating model of an organization. To figure out how to improve our organization's capabilities in developing business insight and using analytics, we need to first know what capabilities we have today. We mentioned the organizational pillars (people, process, technical infrastructure, and culture) as the structural foundation of the organization. The organizational capabilities to produce and consume business insight should be viewed from these four key perspectives. The collective capabilities of all four pillars make up the overall organizational capabilities, including strengths and weaknesses. So, the second requirement of the journey is to recognize that each organization must understand and develop the key pillars together, and then figure out the organization's current collective capabilities.

Establishing a baseline of the organization's current capabilities is the first step in the journey to a higher organizational maturity level. The technical infrastructure pillar typically gets a lot of attention in most cases. It is a critical foundation that any organization needs in order to manage its information assets and develop the insight it needs to make decisions. However, technology alone will not help an organization advance to a more mature and robust state. The other three pillars must be strong and functional to get the most from technology.

In fact, research suggests the "people" component is the most critical pillar of an organization.

In summary, organizations need to establish a baseline of their current capabilities, including strengths and weaknesses in each of the four key organizational pillars, to be able to develop a strategy and roadmap to implement their business transformation. To successfully assess and determine this capabilities baseline, organizations will need a structured approach and methodology. The SAS organizational maturity model (the Information Evolution Model) is used in the following chapters to provide a structured approach to evaluate current organizational capabilities, determine the target destination, and figure out what additional capabilities are needed to get from the starting point to the target organization maturity destination.

ALIGNING CAPABILITIES WITH BUSINESS OBJECTIVES

The third requirement for this business transformation journey is actually the hardest one. If the organization knows the strategic objectives that have been outlined by the executive team and has assessed its current capabilities to establish a baseline, then the only thing left to do is to execute, right? Correct! But we need to keep in mind that this final requirement is not a one-time effort. This final requirement entails changes to the organization's operating model to align its effort in each of the four organizational pillars with the organization's business objectives. This means aligning the hiring and employee performance evaluation practices and incentives. It includes making changes and enhancements to the technical infrastructure, and developing sufficient well-defined processes and engagement models for business units and IT to use. It also must include a change management process to gradually change the organization's culture to use information and the business insight produced by analytics to support decisions and validate strategies. All these changes must be aligned with the organization's strategic objectives.

This alignment is an ongoing process. Many organizations launch these business transformation efforts and actively work on them for some time. Then some lose momentum, get too busy with tactical day-to-day requirements, and undo some of the progress they have made. This is one of the reasons that we need executive support to monitor business performance from an enterprise perspective using the organization's performance management capabilities and take corrective actions when necessary.

Achieving this continuous alignment is not an easy job, and the question is who will take on these additional responsibilities, or how can organizations accelerate this transformation process. An enterprise Center of Excellence can be a very effective method, among other recommendations, to help organizations in accelerating their business transformation effort. The structure and role of an enterprise Center of Excellence are important topics in the discussion of business transformation. These topics are covered in more detail in Chapter 6. It is important to understand that establishing a Center of Excellence is not the only required step in implementing a business transformation plan. Centers of Excellence will accelerate the internal adoption of changes and enhancements that are part of the organization's business transformation plan, and should be viewed from this perspective. Many other changes are necessary to implement business transformation plans.

Aligning an organization is like setting up a tent. Think of people, process, technology, and culture as its four poles. Each pole needs to be equally high or your tent is going to be a bit lopsided. Needless to say, if one pole collapses, you don't have a functioning tent. Or, put another way, the four pillars are like the four wheels of a car. The four wheels must be properly inflated and aligned to optimize your car's performance. And if one of your car's tires is not performing well to match the other three, you may not be able to get to your destination. Organizations don't often view these four criteria equally, and that's when you end up with a mismatch. Particularly common is the situation in which the technology purchased can't be used effectively to show business value because the people, processes, and culture aren't in place to take advantage of it. Another common situation is when organizations lose their highly skilled resources because those people are frustrated by a lack of accurate information and processes to support the business or the lack of a culture that values and uses information to make decisions and set strategies. There are lots of lopsided, partially collapsed tents out there. Let's look at how to build some sturdy tent poles and get them aligned at the same height.

EIGHT WAYS YOU CAN TELL YOU HAVE AN ALIGNMENT ISSUE

1. We invested so much in technology and resources, but we are still struggling with data integration, business silos, and getting a consistent view of our business performance.
2. Business return from our investment is not visible or quantifiable.
3. We can't figure out the right balance between tactical and strategic priorities.
4. We can't produce a 360-degree view of our customers or understand our value chain.
5. We have too many repetitive processes.
6. We can't rationalize or deal with our different competing priorities.
7. The use of our critical resources and talents is not optimized.
8. Given our capabilities and talents, we should have a much better market-competitive advantage.

LET'S START THE JOURNEY

We discussed the three requirements to structure and successfully complete the business transformation journey. Organizations will have to develop a strategy to guide them through that journey. An organizational executive will have to sponsor and own the development and implementation of the strategy. Chapter 7 focuses on how organizations can develop a business transformation strategy.

The second requirement of the business transformation journey is to assess the current organization's capabilities. This process will produce a capabilities baseline that must identify strengths and weaknesses in each of the current four key organizational pillars. This step is necessary to be able to develop a strategy and roadmap to implement their business transformation. The baseline will be used as the starting point for your journey toward a higher organizational maturity level. The second essential requirement is to figure out the target maturity level and its required capabilities. For organizations to complete this task, they need a well-structured and comprehensive approach and methodology.

Chapters 3, 4, and 5 review the SAS Information Evolution Model (IEM), which provides the required methodology to objectively evaluate organizations' maturity levels. The model provides a structured approach to evaluate current organizational capabilities, determine the target destination, and help organizations discover what additional capabilities are needed to get from the starting point to the target organizational maturity destination.

The IEM model[1] has been patented by the U.S. government and has been used effectively to develop the required details for organizational transformations. The model applies to all types of organizations in all industries in the private and public sectors. It focuses on evaluating how organizations develop and consume information and business insights and how they effectively use information to make decisions and validate strategies.

The model describes five organizational maturity levels in the context of the four organizational pillars: people, process, technical infrastructure, and culture. The levels are:

1. Individual
2. Departmental
3. Enterprise
4. Optimize
5. Innovate

Individual is the lowest organizational maturity level, and innovate is the highest. The five levels can be grouped into three key operational categories (see Figure 2.2):

1. Challenged levels (individual and departmental)
2. Foundational level (enterprise)
3. Progressive levels (optimize and innovate)

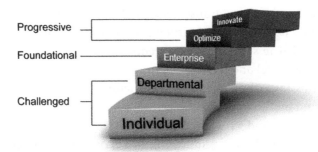

Figure 2.2 Information Evolution Model Levels and Categories

The description and characteristics of these three organization maturity categories are reviewed in greater detail in Chapters 3, 4, and 5.

TAKING THE FIRST STEPS TO TRANSFORMING YOUR ORGANIZATION

W. Edwards Deming put it succinctly: "It is not necessary to change. Survival is not mandatory." It's fascinating to see how many of the quality guru's midcentury musings still hold true today. He was early to identify what today is called "executive sponsorship." Deming's statistical processes for improving quality didn't gain traction in the United States, so when he had the opportunity to work with Japanese industry after World War II he wisely decided to take his ideas straight to the top.

Deming had to export his methods to another continent in order to be heard. We hope you won't have to travel so far. This book explores further the role of people, information processes, technology infrastructure, and culture, the pillars that underpin the SAS Information Evolution Model. And it illustrates the shift from using data tactically to employing it strategically by deriving as much business insight as possible to guide the decision-making process.

NOTE

1. U.S. Patent No 7 752 070 B2.

CHAPTER 3

Challenged Organizations: When Rugged Individualism and Department Silos Aren't Enough

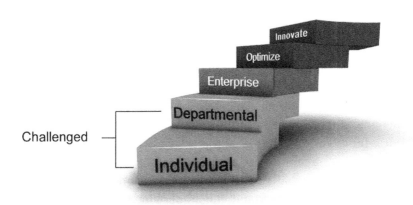

What we've learned so far: People, information processes, technical infrastructure, and culture are the pillars that organizations must strengthen to gain insight from information and use that insight to make sound decisions and validate strategies. The best way to do this is through an understanding of an Information Maturity Model, an unbiased, vendor-neutral approach that allows each organization to craft its own roadmap toward information maturity. The maturity model uses levels that each organization can assess their maturity against.

You might be tempted to skip this chapter, as it describes organizations with significant information maturity issues. You probably don't think your organization is that bad off. Think again. In a recent report, Gartner expects that by 2015 20 percent of Global 1000 organizations will have established a strategic focus on information infrastructure equal to that of application management.[1] That means at least 80 percent of the largest companies don't have that now. Since four out of five of you are likely in these circumstances, reading about the Challenged Level organizations will help you get a better understanding of where you stand today.

Organizations stuck at the Individual Level operate in a near total enterprise data vacuum even if they are churning out a lot of data and reports. Competitiveness and market conditions put them in a precarious state. Organizations whose operations are at the Departmental Level are common across multiple industries and exist around the world. They might be well-led or poorly run, large or small, innovative or staid. Often these organizations have units, brands, regions, and departmental silos that do a great job using their data to produce their own view and perspective of their performance. What they don't have is an enterprise-wide view of business performance. They are at particularly high risk of inadvertently cannibalizing revenue and profits due to their inability to understand their performance across business functions.

What these organizations have in common is that they are at risk. They don't have a complete view of their organization "value chain." They don't understand the underlying metrics that drive their revenue and profits. Both Individual and Departmental organizations are considered challenged, because that verb fits them to a T.

If these challenges sound familiar, you'll want to learn more about how your organization can develop an aggressive roadmap to improve its environment today and start evolving toward a more profitable level of organizational maturity.

GETTING ALONG ONE DAY AT A TIME: ORGANIZATIONS AT THE INDIVIDUAL LEVEL

The business focus of organizations at the Individual Level is on immediate and tactical needs—the here and now. Information gathering evolves to support day-to-day operations. Narrow "stovepipe" applications and transactional systems exist, but they support fragmented business operations.

The executives, managers, and staff of these organizations generally make decisions in unplanned and chaotic information environments. Leaders do not have long-range plans regarding data use nor do they place any value on information standards. As a result, information quality and consistency is questionable. Gut feel, personal experience, and intuition take the place of information as the key factors in decision making. What information is available is often controlled by a "Data Maverick" that you'll learn more about later in this chapter. Luck and visionary leaders are probably the only things keeping these organizations in business.

While these organizations may be profitable at certain stages of the market lifecycle, their low level of information management maturity limits their ability to sustain this success over the long term. These organizations are operating in a very risky environment, and can approach a cliff with unforeseen consequences. Here are a few reasons why:

- Inconsistent views of business performance significantly increase the chance for inaccurate decisions and policies. If you are an Internet retailer offering "free" shipping for some orders, is that a marketing cost? Or does it come off the bottom line?

And is the data being collected in enough detail so you can even tell whether free shipping helps or hurts your organization?

- Reaction time is slowed. When accurate enterprise or even departmental view of performance is lacking, the organization is unable to react effectively to market changes and challenges— economic, competitive, resources, or others. If your organization is tied up trying to consolidate spreadsheets sent in from regional offices all over the globe, it doesn't have time to react to market changes, let alone plot strategy to be proactive.

- Compliance with government audits and regulations is problematic. Expending extra resources and time to make the data comply with government regulations does not help the bottom line, but it is necessary in light of rules like the Basel Accords and the USA Patriot Act.

- Strong candidates leave or avoid your organization. The lack of new talent, coupled with the revolving door of individuals who don't want to deal with Data Mavericks, limits the organization's ability to operate efficiently, innovate, and survive.

- Expansion is difficult and risky. The lack of consistent data, standards, and governance presents significant challenges that hinder the organization's ability to operate in different markets and regions.

Decisions after the Fact

From the 30,000-foot perspective, organizations at the Individual Level are focused on getting the job done today. It's a tactical approach that provides few opportunities to look at the bigger picture. These organizations often end up relying too much on external consultants for strategic projects—and virtually everything is a project. Asking questions like "At what point would we be better off exiting this business?" or "How much money should we spend to gain new customers?" involves at least some significant data gathering and cleansing that is frequently accompanied by a lengthy series of ad hoc steps to hunt down the data and create a report that is out-of-date almost from the moment it arrives on the executive's desk.

True story: When a marketing executive arrived at his new job at a retailer he received a binder that showed the results of an entire year's analytics effort. It said that the best customers were the ones who shopped most frequently. It didn't address what marketing efforts worked or which were the most cost-effective—just a report that stated the obvious.

Being reactive is par for the course. Individual organizations can rarely see micro patterns emerge before they start nibbling at the bottom line. As long as data is perceived as correct for operational purposes—bills are accurate, orders are filled correctly, collections are made promptly (and even that doesn't always happen)—upper-level management is content. For everything else, managers make decisions based on hunches, or what worked at their last company, or maybe what they heard at a conference. And when they decide to find some data—perhaps to justify a hunch—efforts to track down the data meet roadblocks. Maybe the Data Maverick doesn't like the direction of the manager's request so she finds data to shape a narrative of what she thinks is going on. Or maybe the request has to go to the IT department, which puts it in a queue behind the pressing needs of the operational side of the business.

Managers often don't understand how risky the situation is. Not only are these organizations less able to respond to dips in sales or revenue—they can be bowled over by high demand for their service or product. A simple illustration of this is small and mid-sized organizations that book "daily deal" offers through companies like Groupon. Meant to drive new business at a modest marketing cost, only 44 percent of these offers were profitable for restaurants surveyed by a Rice University professor.[2] These organizations often had a hard time figuring out what kind of offer to construct that would not cause them to spend more to staff their operations than they would get back in repeat business at full price. Some actually shut their doors after participation in these offers caused them to lose money or they lost valuable customers paying full price.

To say the least, Individual Level organizations aren't equipped to operate globally. This is due to the fact that a fundamental understanding of the organization's business performance and value chain is lacking at the Enterprise Level. Good understanding of the internal processes, the viability of the organization's products and services, and the organization's interactions and collaboration with its external partners are all essential requirements to enable the organization to operate on a global level. The inability to operate effectively at a global level may limit the organization's competitive advantage. It is a particular burden for financial services companies eager to expand beyond their country of origin. Whether they want to provide banking services to expats, service their customers with business operations in other countries, or simply to export what they see as innovative and well-priced products, information immaturity threatens not just profitability, but it can put them at regulatory risk.

In our current economic and market conditions, these organizations can only survive if they have little or no external market pressure from the competition. Once the pressure increases, Individual Level organizations are forced to look internally at their current operation and evolve their organization to a higher capability level (maturity).

Is your organization functioning at the Individual Level? Let's take a look now at how people, information processes, technical infrastructure, and culture operate at this level.

Rogues Manning the Spreadsheets

In this type of environment, Data Mavericks thrive. These are individuals with the technical skills to work magic with a spreadsheet. They can tell you all about their favorite desktop database, or they know just who to ask in IT—and what to ask for—to gain access to operational systems or get a useable report back.  A department's monthly report, weekly sales figures, or quarterly marketing plan can't make it out the door without the help of this person because no one else can access the information or knows what to do with it.

While some of these individuals try to spread knowledge across the department, often they have wised up to their value and become information hoarders and data gatekeepers. Some grow frustrated quickly and leave for companies with a more mature commitment to being insight driven—leaving a gaping knowledge void in their wake. In organizations mired at the Individual Level, these mavericks are sprinkled across the organization—with multiple mavericks in the biggest business units.

The Data Mavericks are very interested in information because they like to work with data, and they've discovered it's their ticket to life employment, at least as long as your organization stays stuck in a low level of information maturity. If no one else can whip up a report or set of numbers, they're golden. But before you look askance at the data analyst in marketing who figured out how to write Excel programs that trimmed your catalog list without impacting revenue, understand that they are often aided and abetted by managers who haven't a clue how to use data—or are frankly frightened by it.

Dismissive of business intelligence solutions, dashboards, and metric development efforts, Data Mavericks gain a powerful foothold because organizations don't value hiring, motivating, and retaining individuals with critical thinking, technology, and analytics skills outside the IT organization. And the decision makers who manage these individuals are so focused on day-to-day crises that they can't look at matters strategically.

 WHAT ARE DATA MAVERICKS?

Data Mavericks are data-knowledgeable workers who realize the organization is so disorganized when it comes to using data that controlling data is the key to job security.

The existence of Data Mavericks isn't a problem, per se, unless they try to fight off efforts to develop a more mature approach to information gathering. A larger issue in understanding the "people" part of the maturity puzzle is making sure decision makers want to base their decisions on quality information—and that they aren't too comfortable working with Data Mavericks to create information that makes both of them look good at the expense of the greater good of your organization. All that said, probably the best sign that you are operating at the Individual Level is that you can't produce critical reports if you lose certain staff.

INDIVIDUAL LEVEL: PEOPLE

- Happy to share the results, but not the process used to obtain them
- Hostile to unit- or company-wide efforts to establish data processes and governance
- Reluctant to train other employees in data gathering, reporting, and analysis

WHEN "HAVE IT YOUR WAY" ISN'T A GOOD THING

You're in charge of an organization that sells subscriptions for various services. You would like to know the renewal rate. That's a really simple question, right? It should be. For companies at the Individual Level, it's anyone's guess how many different answers you're going to get, or whether the method used to answer the question one year will be the same the next. Most of the effort tends to be ad hoc. Consistent information processes often don't exist. Information is pieced together with lots of queries to IT or through requests to Data Mavericks who make decisions on the fly as to how to interpret the questions and present the data.

When organizations operate at this level they struggle with performance metrics because of their sloppy information processes. On the financial side, there is usually a set of metrics (often standardized

Information Processes

by industry) and information is gathered to report on them. But other types of metrics are generally not collected and used, including information on customer satisfaction, internal efficiencies, and external market conditions. Most of the metrics are lagging metrics; that is, they focus on past performance. Rather than a dashboard with information updated regularly, you get a report that is quickly out of date. IT and data quality governance rarely exist. People who prize autonomy appreciate the lack of standard protocol—it lets them gather and report data in whatever manner suits them. And without documented processes, standards, and policies, nothing is repeatable and any effort to analyze your data becomes a project.

INDIVIDUAL LEVEL: INFORMATION PROCESSES

- There are no department or organization standards policies around data collection so consistent results are rare.
- Metrics are focused on the recent financial performance of the organization, ignoring indicators like customer satisfaction or turnover.
- Developing accurate enterprise business performance views is difficult and time-consuming.
- Information management and data governance, if it exists, is limited to operational and financial systems.

SUPERHIGHWAYS AND DIRT ROADS

It's not all bad news at the Individual Level. There are often strong pockets of technology use, including enterprise resource planning (ERP) and supply chain systems. IT typically has the mission-critical processes running smoothly—from keeping the e-mail virus-free to processing the payroll (if that's done in-house). But

the business performance calculations—the "where are we now and where are we going in the future"—is often powered by a collection of unconnected and unsophisticated desktop and personal productivity tools, such as Microsoft Excel and Access. Everyone has his or her own pool of data, way of analyzing it, and business rules—sometimes his or her own customized tool. Methods are rarely documented, so when the Data Maverick who created the program leaves, the program is orphaned.

If there are no technology standards at the department or Enterprise Level, sharing data is a challenge. If more sophisticated tools are used, it is only because ambitious, self-taught employees have acquired them. Automating the distribution of information to decision makers is not a common practice. Consequently, decision makers frequently rely on instinct. Multiple and inconsistent reports and business views create confusion and redundancy and result in questionable decision quality.

As the hunt for data is often time-consuming, there is very little time to analyze the data. Organizations that have matured and are operating at the Enterprise Level frequently report that the biggest difference (other than just having accurate, reliable data available) is that they now have time to analyze data.

It's also very tough for the Individual Level organization to take advantage of new technologies. With such a scattered ad hoc infrastructure, it would be difficult to calculate how much money you could save using cloud computing, for instance. Master data management and service-oriented architecture are beyond the ability of the organization to use effectively. You can forget about analyzing Big Data. But even smaller efforts can be problematic. A hotel chain, for instance, might want to use text analytics to monitor online comments. It could outsource the effort—but without mature information processes in-house it can't sync up the information it's receiving (complaints about front desk staff, product quality, or marketing offers) with internal information and then get the right information to the right people to quickly fix the problem—or even determine the severity of complaints and how they should be addressed.

INDIVIDUAL LEVEL: TECHNICAL INFRASTRUCTURE

- A strong operational system in some areas but too much reliance on personal productivity tools, such as Excel and Access. More sophisticated intelligence tools can be orphaned if their user leaves the organization.

- Occasional use of analytics by individuals with the appropriate skills to meet ad hoc business requests. The quality or the results are questionable.

- Proper data management is not a business priority and is haphazardly applied by Data Mavericks.

- Organizations can't take advantage of advances such as master data management, service-oriented architecture, and cloud computing or big data.

- Basic technical infrastructure foundation to support effective data integration, business intelligence, analytics, and performance management is missing.

A Little Too Much Rugged Individualism

The words and phrases that have positive connotations in many cultures—"maverick," "rugged individualism," and "gut instinct"—are not necessarily positive when it comes to working with data. This doesn't mean that a mature information organization is run by humorless statisticians crunching numbers in an effort to stamp out all signs of creativity. Instead, it's using data effectively to foster creativity—and that's not what is happening at the Individual Level. Instead, these organizations have a culture that allows chaos.

You try to reward people for the right reasons, but in Individual Level organizations, people tend to be rewarded for all the wrong reasons. These are the people politically aligned to a certain decision maker, or whose "gut" bet paid off big (even if it may

have cannibalized profit because this organization often doesn't know what drives profit), or who are seen as "indispensable." In this politically charged organization, managers exercise a lot of command and control. Although they issue edicts, the Data Mavericks hold the day-to-day power, since they hold the key to the information that managers need. The environment is internally competitive. Thought leaders and innovators who propose anything "outside the box" are not encouraged or rewarded. They may, in fact, be viewed as a threat. And even if the situation is chaotic, the culture doesn't really like change.

Internal top-down communication is limited, and may only focus on providing general direction or financial targets.

 INDIVIDUAL LEVEL: CULTURE

- Rewards are subjective and often political, focused on individual excellence in day-to-day activities rather than contributions to corporate-level objectives.
- Information practices aren't aligned with the corporate mission and objectives.
- Business units aren't encouraged to share data, and they rarely do.
- Change is feared and shunned unless there is personal gain involved.
- There is little internal collaboration within and between business units.
- Outside-the-box thinking is discouraged.

This bunker mindset at the Individual Level tends to reward personal or product successes without analyzing their impact on other products or unknowingly undermines enterprise-wide profitability. Because success depends on the efforts of one or two talented workers, the organization's ability to identify and repeat successful information processes, products, or services is limited, especially if key personnel leave.

The ironic aspect is all the money that Individual Level organizations save by not investing in people and infrastructure costs indirectly in lost opportunity. Organizations at this level will sometimes invest in technologies to deal with data volume, or attempt to solve a problem because a Data Maverick convinced management a new solution was needed. But without consistent validation, quality standards, governance—and a culture populated with individuals ready to act on data—the technology investment is for naught. These organizations are the most likely to "turn off" an expensive investment because the groundwork wasn't prepared to effectively use it.

What is the most unfortunate thing about operating at the Individual Level? So few recognize that they are. Too often, organizations at this level face a major crisis that forces them to quickly evolve—an expensive and wrenching experience. Better to take a proactive approach to candidly identify their level before that happens.

CONSOLIDATED, BUT NOT COHESIVE: ORGANIZATIONS AT THE DEPARTMENTAL LEVEL

An interesting dilemma occurred around a convention booking at a resort hotel. The hotel's convention and marketing units were becoming increasingly savvy about using data to create offers. There was only one problem—they never worked together. Rates were assigned by a revenue management system. Both the marketing and the convention units were looking for slow periods to market more heavily, when there would be plenty of rooms available at a low rate. And they both independently locked on a specific weekend. A large convention was booked, rooms were blocked, but when individual travelers called to get the special rate created by marketing they were met with an "I'm sorry; we don't have any rooms available at that rate." Marketing's time and expenses were wasted, and instead of making customers happy, they ticked them off.

Business units at this level don't ask: "How will this decision affect the organization as a whole?" They ask: "How will my department's metrics look better?" Unlike the Individual Level organization, these businesses often have entire departments that are savvy about using data, follow solid processes for working with and

governing data, and take a team approach. Data Mavericks have been induced to play team ball. These are organizations that boast marketing departments that understand the total value of a customer or warranty groups that have slashed costs and optimized processes.

The problem is that data is stored and analytic applications are designed, developed, and supported from a departmental perspective without much consideration for how well those data might integrate with other units in the enterprise. As business units at the Departmental Level continue to act and think locally, the enterprise will end up with many information silos, each with its own version of the truth.

By becoming subject matter experts with regard to the information under their control, these business units tend to use their information access for political power and may even go so far as to shield the department from scrutiny at the enterprise reporting level. In many cases, enterprise goals and objectives are secondary to departmental goals, so much so that they may be tracked manually or not at all. To reach any enterprise-level decision or attempt to gain any enterprise-wide perspective, these conflicting silos of information must be painstakingly merged and rationalized. It is not uncommon for organizations at this level to have sophisticated data gathering and reporting abilities at the unit level—and for those units to then cut and paste their results into a spreadsheet that someone in a C-level executive's office must try to reconcile and synthesize.

In fairness, there are data-savvy groups aware of the possibilities that exist if they can integrate data with other units in the enterprise. They often report that significant roadblocks exist that they are not equipped to break down.

SUBJECT MATTER EXPERTS AND GATEKEEPERS

The Data Mavericks who agreed to be team players have migrated to jobs with titles like business analyst. Although the business units may have data governance and processes in place these analysts still spend a lot of time preparing and integrating information,

and, if no automated business intelligence system is available, more time is needed to develop reports that put the best departmental spin on the data. Note the word "spin." There still tends to be a lot of emphasis on using data to match a business unit's expectations versus reality. In other words, if the marketing department invested a lot of money in a specific advertising medium, they're going to look for data points to justify that expense.

Business analysts in the consolidated organization are valued and paid for their information skills. In some cases, they've built up shadow IT empires that clash with an organization's actual IT operation. In addition, a key differentiator between organizations at the Departmental Level and those at the Enterprise Level is that investment in resources, hardware, and training is usually funded by business units to satisfy departmental needs rather than any enterprise program for information and skills development.

The good news is that team players thrive in this type of organization. They have strong managers who defend the department and create internal cohesion. Those with an interest in information management are recognized and appreciated for their skills. The bad news is that the business unit-centric model tends to make it difficult for these individuals to work cooperatively with other departments. After all, those are competitors in the internal corporate struggle for power, recognition, and budget. If someone suggests a Center of Excellence to help create a more enterprise-wide method of dealing with data, the business units are likely to resist, fearing that their budgets or autonomy will be compromised.

DEPARTMENTAL LEVEL: PEOPLE

- Team players for their department; hesitant to work across department lines.
- Training focuses on improving department performance.
- Data gathering and interpretation reflect business unit goals.
- Few skills to support the development and improvement of the enterprise technical architecture.
- Less than effective use of critical skills across the organization.

Strong Interior, Weak Exterior

At this level, information is collected, assembled, accessed, and tracked on a Departmental Level. Data management processes are fairly well defined within each department but not across departments. Since analysis is based on a myopic view, it will not accurately reflect influences from outside the department. Sales and marketing, for instance, might be working with a similar set of numbers but reporting and analyzing them differently. Duplication of effort is common.

Even the simplest things, such as the definition of a "customer" or "sale," can vary by business unit. Standardizing business rules across all the brands to better analyze costs is difficult and politically challenging. For example, if you charge for shipping, should that be revenue or should that be considered part of the cost? At one multichannel retailer, every brand defined it differently.

There is also a heavy focus on static reporting of operational measures, such as gross margins, total revenue, total expense, or inventory on hand. Business analysts perform some interactive analysis to distill other performance measures, but only at a Departmental Level.

If enforced, enterprise rules are left to interpretation by individual departments. Because these departments do maintain individual standards, they are pretty good at outsourcing functions (just like they are fairly good at finding their own technology providers). But just like with technology purchases, there is little corporate governance of this activity, limiting the advantages for economies of scale and consistent quality and vendor management.

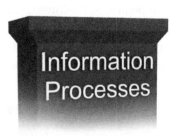

 DEPARTMENTAL LEVEL: INFORMATION PROCESSES

- Data management and governance well-defined at the department level
- No processes in place to support collaboration between business units to agree on standard or on how to interpret enterprise-wide rules

- Strong documentation of processes within departments
- Limited, time-consuming, and often manual processes to produce enterprise business performance view

Many Roads, Not Enough Bridges

There are some enterprise-wide approaches at Departmental Level organizations. Hardware and networking standards have been established across the enterprise, but each department prefers to use its own tools and data standards. Except for basic organization technical infrastructure, there are no enterprise-wide technology standards or frameworks. There might be dozens of departmental databases on servers stored in offices and maintained by individuals, most of them unknown to IT and some even unsupported by the central IT department or their vendors.

At this level, each department acquires and uses its own business intelligence tools—niche or proprietary solutions that address a specific function, such as campaign management, supplier evaluation, or budgeting. These tools might be quite sophisticated, but they cannot be used for broader applications outside the department. Without the oversight or control of an enterprise architecture group, redundancy of tools and applications is both a problem and an added expense. Moving to the next maturity level (Enterprise Level) may force business units to comply with the organization's IT standards or justify the use of their favorite applications to increase the overall return from existing technologies.

Individuals within a department typically have ready access to data for their department. Departmental data marts assemble data from the group's users and make it available in numerous reports, but these reports often present conflicting results across departments and provide limited enterprise context. For instance,

marketing might be measuring the overall success of campaigns—the "lift" rates—but can they follow how the lift rate impacts the company's bottom line? One multichannel retailer, with multiple brands, discovered that discount coupons offered in one catalog cannibalized sales for another brand when it began taking an enterprise-wide view of its information. In addition, offering discount coupons on websites tends to draw in customers who buy one item with no deeper loyalty to the retailer. Finally, they realized that customers who discover the retailer through comparison shopping engines are rarely worth further promotion. This wouldn't work if brands kept their own information silos.

Departmental Level organizations aren't known for sharing information across business units. Needed information might be owned by other departments, and there is no formal way of accessing it. There is some collaboration via meetings, memos, and simple file sharing. But understanding the data still requires the tribal knowledge and goodwill of information gatekeepers. There is too much time spent finding, assembling, and debating the interpretation of information; too little time is spent making sense of it.

If standards aren't kept across silos, even efforts to get departments to share information are likely to fail. For example, the technical infrastructure may define customers, suppliers, and partners differently or use different account codes across departments. Enterprise master data is not well managed.

Departmental Level organizations can adapt to cutting-edge technologies within business units. High-speed analytics, for instance, is possible. But realizing a technology's full enterprise value requires more effort. Financial institutions have to calculate risk exposure across an enterprise and many have embraced high performance analytics to do that quickly—dropping the time to calculate loan defaults from several days to four hours. But if a mortgage group is doing that independently of commercial loans and that group is working independently of consumer loans, what happens when it is time to look at overall risk? Out come the electronic scissors, the virtual paste, and the spreadsheets.

In the area of text analytics, a marketing department might do a fabulous job of determining exactly what consumers like and dislike about a product. But without an enterprise approach, the exercise is just that—an exercise. The marketers can send their report to the warranty, manufacturing, and product development units, but their data might be telling them something different. "We're not getting reports that the buttons are sticky," warranty will say. "Sticky buttons are a warranty problem," says manufacturing. "Our data shows people like those buttons," says product development.

By comparison, in Enterprise Level organizations, the technical infrastructure is capable of analyzing consumer comments and distributing them to all stakeholder groups who will collaborate in analyzing the results. Warranty could mine its own data to look for claims that relate to "sticky buttons" (but aren't called that), manufacturing can look for root causes, sales can track whether sticky button chatter is impacting sales, and product development can begin looking for a workaround at the next stage.

DEPARTMENTAL LEVEL: TECHNICAL INFRASTRUCTURE

- Fragmented hardware and storage—dozens of department databases on servers stored in business unit offices or maintained by individuals aren't uncommon.
- Departments choose their own business intelligence and analytics tools. Redundancy of tools and applications is a problem.
- Enterprise technical infrastructure is expensive to maintain and hard to scale.
- Information access within a department is fine; between departments it is problematic.
- Each department defines key master data its own way, making it difficult to integrate information at the Enterprise Level.

"Us versus Them"

The rewards in a Departmental Level organization revolve strictly around the success of a given unit, brand, or department. These units become expert at using data as "proof" of localized needs and accomplishments. Incentives are based on meeting departmental goals, which may or may not be in line with the best interests of the enterprise.

Change is embraced when it results in political or self-improvement gain for the department—or if it takes place in someone else's department (especially if it creates an opportunity to gain more resources). Change is viewed as a threat if it disrupts the department's own carefully groomed processes or if it requires disparate functional units to work together. Departments might actively resist change that benefits other groups or distracts them from their own missions, even if the company as a whole would benefit. Even under the best of circumstances, change is poorly communicated, cautiously approached, and limited in results.

One of the worst features of Departmental Level organizations is a tendency to assume that if the business units are individually meeting goals, then the enterprise will meet its goals. And if business units aren't meeting goals? Well, they'll argue individually for more money and support. You can see where this is headed. It's the Monday morning meeting where the heads of each business unit present their own version of the truth in the board meeting with the C-level executives and squabble for additional resources. And worse, these organizations don't know what the truth is because there is no one with information that isn't enmeshed in a unit or department. It's "us" versus "them" to the nth degree. The unfortunate consequence of this is the inability of the executive team to make accurate and timely decisions based on well integrated and agreed upon enterprise performance information. They may eventually generate the correct and required information, but it is usually too late and some decisions may have already been made based on gut feeling or intuition.

DEPARTMENTAL LEVEL: CULTURE

- Data used to prove departmental needs and accomplishments.
- Not enough communication and performance measurements to encourage and demand internal collaboration.
- Change is embraced if it furthers a department's goal; not the organization's.
- A politically charged and distrustful situation exists between departments.

The "everyone is in it for themselves" mentality that grips Departmental Level organizations is obviously damaging. The decision that best benefits my group might be gained at your expense. The high cost to maintain the organization's technical infrastructure will continue to grow, allowing more duplication of efforts, hardware, and technology. The inconsistency in coding and maintaining the master data and in storing critical information will continue to introduce challenges in integrating data from various business units. Since the organization is challenged by its inability to develop and analyze its business performance at the Enterprise Level, inaccurate decisions and strategies are made and adopted. You can't achieve a competitive advantage in the market, and deal with market changes and challenges, working in this level.

Failure to see the big picture really poses problems during an economic downturn or when faced with competition that is savvier about gaining insights from information. Root cause analysis for the failure of something—a new product or long-existing popular product—is compromised by never-ending rounds of finger pointing. And businesses operating at the Departmental Level are hamstrung during merger and acquisition discussions by not fully understanding their organizational value chain. If they buy a company and let it work as another silo, they create a problem. If they buy a company and try to integrate operations, the level of information discord can be eye opening.

The good news is that these organizations often possess almost everything necessary to have a unified, enterprise-wide view of information. There is data talent capable of playing for a team and technologies are used that yield strong results. It takes leadership and guts—but not gut instinct—to get to the next level. Let's find out how.

UNDERSTANDING THE TRUE CONSEQUENCES OF THE CHALLENGED LEVELS

It is difficult, frankly, to get many companies to understand what level they are at and why it is such a problem. Many of today's successful executives climbed the corporate ladder before there was even that much data to be had. Their leadership, strong gut instinct, and boldness in moving their organizations into new areas was done in a less competitive environment—certainly as it pertains to information. The Individual Level organizations are, to some extent, more aware of issues because executives who ask a simple question and can get no answers are aware of the problem. Even when getting conflicting answers at the Department Level organizations, executives often figure that this is less an institutional problem than a little turf fighting between departments. If putting an end to those conflicting answers (by moving to the Enterprise Level) involves draining internal battles, maybe a few conflicting answers is a small price to pay. Increasingly, this just won't suffice. Maybe the best way to muster up the courage to face down the silos is to see what an Enterprise Level organization looks like.

BUSINESS TRANSFORMATION STRATEGY OBJECTIVES FOR CHALLENGED ORGANIZATIONS

In Chapter 2, three requirements were described for organizations to successfully embark on a business transformation journey. Organizations will need to develop a business transformation strategy, sponsored by the executive team, to adequately address the three requirements and gradually transform the organization. Chapter 7 is dedicated to the strategy discussions. The strategy will depend on the maturity level of your organization. If you believe your organization has the symptoms and characteristics just described as associated with Challenged organizations, the following should be key objectives for your business transformation strategy:

- Assess your current organization capabilities in the four key pillars to determine which maturity level your organization is operating on and determine capability gaps.

- Identify critical business areas with the highest information and organizational challenges as well as the highest potential business value.

- Leverage your current key talents and resources as part of your strategy. Although they may not be operating in the most efficient manner, they still have significant knowledge of the business.

NOTES

1. Roxane Edjlali, Regina Casonato, Ted Friedman, Mark A. Beyer, and Donald Fineberg, "Predicts 2013: Big Data and Information Infrastructure," Gartner, November 30, 2012, www.gartner.com/document/2258415?ref=QuickSearch&sthkw=Predicts%202013%3A%20Big%20Data%20and%20Information%20Infrastructure.
2. Utpal Dholakia, "How Businesses Fare With Daily Deals As They Gain Experience: A Multi-Time Period Study of Daily Deal Performance Fair," June 2012, http://news.rice.edu/wp-content/uploads/2012/07/2012-07-05-DailyDeals.pdf.

CHAPTER 4

Foundational Organizations: Making the Leap to an Enterprise-Wide Approach

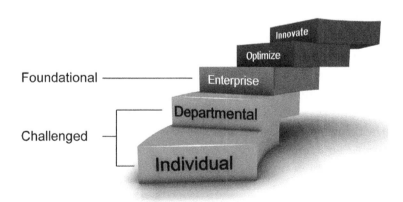

What we've learned so far: Challenged organizations stuck at the Individual or Department levels face multiple hurdles when it comes to developing and using information to help the organization succeed. Individual Level organizations are so focused on immediate tactical needs that they rarely operate strategically. Departmental Level organizations often use information in sophisticated ways, but that information is used to make the department perform better without consideration for the organization as a whole. There is never "one version of the truth." Instead, there are multiple silos and competing versions of the truth.

Will you be in business in five years? Organizations at the Challenged Levels can't say that with certainty. Given the increasing level of market and product competitiveness, improvements in communications and online selling, and the ease with which consumers can research products, organizations must integrate their data across the enterprise to compete aggressively. There is no magic in reaching the Enterprise Level, as you'll learn. It is about building a foundation from which you can develop accurate and consistent enterprise information and can better deploy predictive analytics, big data advances, and optimization techniques in highly competitive and innovative ways.

Moving to the Enterprise Level requires patience and self-awareness. It demands executive-level sponsorship. Achieving this level of organization maturity requires executives who understand the value of an enterprise-wide view of business performance, and are eager to embrace change. More so than even in the preceding levels, making this leap requires more than just technology—key challenges associated with people, processes, and culture must be addressed. This level is the tipping point in the organization's information evolution and signifies the beginning of the evolutionary journey toward higher levels of competitiveness and, ultimately, organizational transformation.

THE POSSIBILITIES THAT COME WITH PATIENCE

The payoffs might not be as obvious—at least not initially. Much of the low-hanging fruit wins in specific departments (more efficient marketing, improvements in handling warranty claims) have happened at the Department Level. The major gains associated with the Enterprise Level occur when organizations develop a good understanding of their value chain for the first time, and start using it to move toward optimization and beyond. This is the level when eyes are opened, synergies knit together, and activities—the acquisition of a competitor, the opening of stores in another country, the streamlining of a supply chain—can be done with more efficiency and ease. That's because Enterprise Level organizations are working with one version of the truth and an informed view of operations across the enterprise. Access to information is uniform and enterprise-wide, and information processes are repeatable. This view of the enterprise is built on the back of enterprise-wide standards and uses an enterprise information architecture that is agile, scalable, and integrated.

SEEING THE VALUE ACROSS THE ENTERPRISE

Everything—including technical infrastructure, people, processes, and culture—is consistent and repeatable at this level. It's all about how you manage the data, not necessarily where you store it or what architecture approach you chose. Thus, a single enterprise data warehouse, multiple smaller data warehouses, or data marts are all options. The key is that the data is consistent across divisions and departments to enable all units to share the same business definitions and use the same metadata. This is possible because the other three organizational pillars are aligned and support the need to have a consistent enterprise view of business performance.

At the Enterprise Level, for the first time, decision makers across the organization can actually see relationships across functions and understand how the organization performs as a whole. Employees can see how their work fits into the big picture. The organization

quickly focuses on defining its value chain, a fundamental requirement for achieving this maturity level.

 WHAT IS A VALUE CHAIN?

The value chain encompasses the points at which value is created when producing, distributing, and servicing a product.
These points might include the acquisition of the raw goods,
the manufacturing of a finished product or service, the identification of sales channels through which to sell the products and
services, and the means of servicing the product or supporting
the customer. No two value chains are alike, and it is incumbent
on organizations to define their chain—a process made immea-
surably easier with an enterprise-wide data view.

The enterprise architecture links information needs and requirements to organizational objectives, and therefore information projects have higher business adoption and success rates. By being able to
identify and document the value chain at the Enterprise Level, organizations can quickly identify what is running well and what needs
to be improved in the next level, the Optimization Level. The analysis
might even show what might be outsourced as a noncore activity. A
value chain analysis might help a manufacturer in the next maturity
level to discover that a low-cost part isn't saving money because of the
costs associated with finishing it (or replacing the finished product). A
bank's value chain analysis could unearth evidence that the customers it thought were most profitable aren't, making it counterproductive to keep offering those customers special deals.

 OVERCOMING WARINESS

Challenged organizations are often wary of seeking the
Enterprise Level as they think it means relinquishing all infor-
mation and analytical endeavors to a centralized organization.
Business units sometimes see it as a power grab, or complain
that the Enterprise Level effort will return them to the Dark
Ages of having to get in line for simple reports. Neither is the

case. At the Enterprise Level, there is a balance between business unit autonomy and enterprise requirements. At this level, organizations establish business and IT standards that guide information and technical architecture and provide organization-wide performance metrics and definitions. Business units have the flexibility to manage their operations within this framework. No one seeks to confiscate analytical productivity tools. Rather, Enterprise Level organizations care about the underlying information moving in and out of the tools.

What else can an Enterprise Level organization do that Challenged organizations can't? Let's start with a few simple examples: agreeing on what a customer is, which products are profitable, and who the organization's suppliers are (all of them, with subsidiaries mapped). If you've ever attempted to get answers to these questions at a Challenged organization you know it (a) took much too long and (b) involved different answers from different business units. Identifying basic value chain information is essential and places the organization at the tipping point to focus on optimization and innovation in the next higher maturity levels.

But what about those "aha" moments reached at the Department Level? The application that increased the efficiency of marketing spend or helped make sense of the supply chain? These "wins" are real. At the Enterprise Level, the aha moments transcend department-specific metrics and speak to the goals of the organization as a whole. At Department Level organizations, the manufacturing unit might consider a product profitable, while the warranty department is reporting it isn't. Marketing might consider its efforts to tout a service successful, while finance is seeing diminished profit on higher sales. It's an enterprise-wide view of the data that quickly reveals the problems that led one department to think it hit a home run while another department is shaking its head. Or better yet, it keeps the problems from occurring in the first place. With an enterprise-wide view of the data, marketing and finance can work together to model likely profit outcomes of a new service plan *before they offer it.*

You might be thinking, "Oh, we have found unprofitable marketing efforts and product defects that hurt the bottom line. We've even modeled outcomes before introducing a product or service—and no one made us reach this Enterprise Level." Of course you did, but how hard was it? How long did it take? Would you say you did this reactively or proactively? And how often have your C-level executives disagreed over whether something was truly profitable? At the Enterprise Level, for the first time, organizations can efficiently, proactively, and confidently use data to drive decisions that benefit the entire organization.

HOW AN ENTERPRISE LEVEL ORGANIZATION FUNCTIONS

So what does this Enterprise Level really look like? These organizations get the strategic and competitive value of information and work as one entity, not a disparate group of business units. To that end:

- Enterprise business performance is the main focus and driver. There is now a set of common corporate strategies and tactics, and each group understands its role in executing those tactics and the correlation among business units. Performance is now managed based on an informed, comprehensive view of all operations across the enterprise.

- Information is seen as a critical strategic asset, just as important as tangible, operational assets. Everyone understands that integrated information is essential to run the business. The organization has managed to integrate internal and external information successfully across business units and functions to create an enterprise view of the operation.

- For the first time, the organization understands its business value chain. Managers and staff also appreciate the importance of data quality.

- Integrated enterprise information is now available to all decision makers across the enterprise, and around the globe. Decisions are focused around managing the value chain, such as engaging new suppliers or launching campaigns to support dormant markets.

While clean data is tapped for use in specific analytics efforts, the Enterprise Level organization is driven on a daily basis by Key

Performance Indicators (KPIs) that have been developed with input across the enterprise. When developing KPIs, it is important to know that:

- People across all business units of the enterprise have discussed and agreed on the business performance KPIs.
- Processes are designed to make sure the KPIs are produced and distributed using the right data for the metric.
- Information is made available in a timely fashion and technology is employed to that end.
- The culture accepts the metrics and uses them to drive decisions and reward people.

All the pillars are in alignment. Now let's visit each pillar in more detail.

Knowledge Workers Equipped with the Right Information and Technologies

At the Enterprise Level, anyone who needs to make a decision has access to information. Decision makers can identify alternatives and act on information from a truly enterprise-wide perspective, and their decisions reflect enterprise goals and objectives. Marketing, for example, might be responsible primarily for getting more click-throughs on a website. They have access to the click-through rates, but also have access to whether the click-throughs are leading to sales, which come from the sales business units. And if they aren't, the marketing department is empowered to redesign offers to drive sales. They aren't measured on an isolated metric—click-throughs, with resultant sales being, well, a sales problem. Is marketing taking the blame for poor sales? Not at all. Because at this level, marketing can see that the high click-throughs/low sales are coming from products that aren't available (a fulfillment problem). In a siloed operation, marketing would be rewarded for creating emails and websites that spawn high click-throughs while the unit responsible for making sure product

was available would be judged on its overall fulfillment levels. In an Enterprise organization, both units would need to work together to meet a KPI measuring click-throughs to sales. Each unit would be acknowledged for what it accomplished for the organization, not what it accomplished in a vacuum.

Enterprise Level organizations have a high percentage of knowledge workers—team players who have domain knowledge and understand corporate goals. Career development programs are well established and widely used to keep employees current with new skills, technologies, and best practices. Marketing staff have more than just career development programs aimed at juicing their creativity. They are also trained on how to measure their successes and use available data to make decisions. These organizations don't promote or reward the data averse.

ENTERPRISE LEVEL: PEOPLE

- Recruited with targeted technical, analytical, and information skills. The workforce contains a high percentage of "knowledge workers."

- Team players who have domain expertise and understand corporate goals are the norm. Interdepartmental competitiveness fades and collaboration is encouraged.

- Exceptional information skills are retained and rewarded because the organization places a high value on information.

No More KPI Confusion

Where an organization gets its data, how it enters its systems, and how it is cleaned, stored, and used is monitored and guided at the Enterprise Level. Business units still own their information, but processes are in place to integrate business unit information, produce

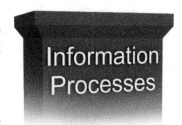

enterprise performance views, and share them across the enterprise. Proper information management concepts and best practices are applied and accepted. Data management processes are well defined, resulting in a shared view of operations and a reliable foundation for analysis. Processes to obtain information are well defined and detailed—technologies, people, plans, tasks, and responsibilities. Data is governed: A sale is tracked the same way regardless of who booked it. The same goes for orders, raw materials, and supplies.

Now that the organization has a holistic view of the enterprise, it starts to see duplicate, overlapping, and inefficient processes. In Departmental Level organizations, problems with customer retention might trickle down to the business units that would then embark independently on analytic projects to figure out what is going on. The Call Center unit might be pinging IT looking for data on transactions that occurred between the customer and call center prior to the customer switching to a competitor. Another unit might be building a model to look at what customers buy in the six months before they drop their service so they can predict who might be leaving and provide a special offer. These expensive, time-consuming efforts might yield conflicting suggestions (especially if the underlying data is inconsistent). In contrast, Enterprise Level organizations might build a model across the business units looking at all customer interactions in the six months before they left so business units aren't left pointing fingers at each other, but instead working collaboratively to figure out the root cause of customer attrition and the best way to improve their efforts.

 OUTSOURCING AT THE ENTERPRISE LEVEL

Organizations are often advised to outsource activities that are not part of their core competencies. But without an enterprise-wide view of data, it can be difficult to outsource cost-effectively. Individual units might be negotiating separate contracts with the same vendors. There might be no standards or processes for choosing which business functions to outsource, and no effort to make sure critical data generated from the outsourcing looped back to the business. In Enterprise Level organizations, these processes are standardized, and controls are in place for the bidirectional movement of data and information to and from vendors.

ENTERPRISE LEVEL: INFORMATION PROCESSES

- Enterprise information governance is enforced, and data consistency is paramount.
- Centers of Excellence are used to help promote and ensure consistent data definitions, data collection, data quality, analytics, and information delivery.
- Departmental and business unit information processes align with enterprise objectives and with each other.
- Data stewards are identified, and the organization has control of its critical enterprise master data.
- The organization is better able to comply with external reporting requirements, such as Sarbanes-Oxley, Basel II, IFRS, GAAP, SEC, Solvency II, FDA, and other regulatory bodies.

Freedom of Choice Knitted into a Sound Framework

The Enterprise Level organization doesn't dictate which analytical tools to use. Rather, there is a concerted effort to manage and rationalize tools across departments and business units. In this environment, an organization might decide it is more cost-effective to place tools and solutions on a server, rather than keeping them on each desktop. It might consolidate around certain vendors—keeping "best of breed" technologies where necessary. Value to the organization does trump an individual user's comfort level with a tool or solution, but there is no bureaucratic sweep to rid the enterprise of anything but a select group of tools or solutions.

 ## JUST SAY NO TO THE BLACK BOX

Enterprise-wide organizations know what is under the hoods of the analytical tools they use. At this level, "black box" tools that promise to spit out an answer if certain data is fed into the "box" are dropped in favor of tools whose logic is relevant and understood by the sophisticated knowledge workers populating Enterprise Level organizations.

While the analytical tools are diverse, the organization tends to use a standardized set of technologies to manage data integration, distribution, and reporting. Now that information resides in central data repositories, it is available to decision makers at all levels of the organization, not just the original data "owners" or the executives. Information access and security is also managed from an enterprise perspective. Furthermore, the information has been cleansed through standard data-quality routines, so users can have confidence in the results. Decision makers now have access to information that represents "one version of the truth," presented to them with contextual relevance.

Users have access to the data through interfaces tailored for their specific needs and skill sets. Data can be organized and analyzed regardless of whether it is structured or unstructured. Trending on social media is captured along with sales data. Executive dashboards, summary information with drill-down capability for business managers, ad hoc query for business analysts, and sophisticated model development for quantitative analysts are examples of the flexibility provided. It is fairly easy for the organization to add visual options and move data to mobile applications. As a result, more users than ever can access and explore information with confidence that they can make more accurate decisions.

Analysts who were once stuck using only the data they could get from their business unit now have near real-time access to enterprise data. They are also freed from tedious data collection and preparation activities, allowing them time to extract insight from data.

ENTERPRISE LEVEL: TECHNICAL INFRASTRUCTURE

- Enterprise and business unit requirements drive the organization's information infrastructure.

- An information model and architecture relevant to the organization's industry and specific business is used to structure and maintain enterprise information.

- Enterprise information architecture is dynamic to accommodate business changes and scalable to incorporate the increased availability of external and unstructured information.

- Clean and consistent enterprise information provides the organization with the ability to take advantage of advances in "Big Data" analysis, high-performance analytics, cloud computing, mobile computing, and text analytics using enterprise data.

- The adoption of new technologies is a managed process at the enterprise level. The organization is systematic in how technology is acquired, deployed, and maintained while still allowing departments to retain necessary autonomy to meet their individual business needs.

All for One, One for All

Business units in highly evolved Departmental organizations may question the necessity of reaching the Enterprise Level. The resource competition that exists at Departmental organizations can be spun as a positive. Or they might feel that moving to the Enterprise Level implies a level of micromanagement that stifles innovation. Those of you who have identified your organizations as Departmental

Level might be thinking, "Can't our business units simply share their successes with other business units?" Others might think the issue of information not being in sync when it reaches the top of the organization is inevitable in a large enterprise. These are excuses. There is no long-term value to staying at the Departmental Level. Furthermore, Departmental Level organizations are reactive and are at a disadvantage when they need to compete with innovative products and services.

That said, multidisciplinary teamwork is the hallmark of the Enterprise Level organization, and teams frequently pop up to work on corporate-wide issues. Employees may be temporarily assigned to cross-departmental teams in a way that best utilizes their skills and job functions. The goal, of course, is to not create queue-producing "projects" but ongoing processes that feed analytics-driven insights to decision makers.

When an organization truly reaches this Enterprise Level, everyone is focused on the health of the enterprise and on producing high-quality data and analysis for strategic value. The organization shows its understanding of the information value by funding efforts to manage enterprise information and acquire and retain critical talents. Issues that had sat on the back burner, such as efforts to measure and improve social responsibility and sustainability, can be undertaken with ease and efficiency.

ENTERPRISE LEVEL: CULTURE

- The organization is managed based on an informed understanding of the enterprise value chain.
- Business priorities are used to measure employee performance and provide incentives.
- There is more emphasis on critical thinking and analytical skills, with talent made available for cross-departmental initiatives.
- The availability of reliable enterprise information is feeding data-driven decision making.

BIG DATA: THE BIG OPPORTUNITY FOR ENTERPRISE LEVEL ORGANIZATIONS

Big data provides organizations the ability to apply modeling and analytics to large and detailed amounts of data. In the past, analysts relied on sampling, summarizing, and categorizing data to reduce its size before analytics could be applied. Departmental Level organizations with functioning silos can certainly benefit from the boon in technologies that make it easier to analyze large volumes of all related data, not subsets. But Enterprise Level organizations are better poised to maximize the benefit from big data analysis by applying this technology to enterprise information versus departmental information.

For example, big data allows retailers to forecast, measure, and model their consumer price sensitivity with much finer granularity than in the past. Now retailers are able to do it at the store level, by a stock-keeping unit (SKU) level, or by a unit of time. In the past, this type of analysis was limited to higher grouping and categorizations of products and regions. An Enterprise Level organization has already integrated its data and can use big data analytics much more effectively than a Departmental Level organization. Departmental Level organizations can (and do) use big data analysis on their own efforts, but the impact for the enterprise is limited. For example, financial institutions' risk departments are increasingly taking advantage of big data to make better decisions about investments and loans. But if the information isn't integrated across the enterprise, other departments could be working at cross purposes. A marketing push for a certain kind of loan could lead to thousands of upset customers who discover, once the prospective loan is analyzed by the risk department, that they won't qualify.

Being able to generate more business insight from enterprise information adds a competitive advantage for Enterprise Level organizations that can produce better financial performance, and enables organizations to be proactive in predicting market trends.

DON'T LET UP

The risks facing the Challenged Level organizations are quite clear (as detailed in Chapter 2), but there are risks in reaching the Enterprise

Level as well. In order to succeed at this level, organizations must (1) use the information generated, (2) act on it effectively, and (3) avoid the temptation to backslide. That last one is big—because organizations often lose sight of a fundamental aspect of information maturity: It's not a one-and-done project. In fact, market research done by SAS indicates that the majority of organizations are stuck between the Departmental Level and the Enterprise Level. "We've integrated our data, we've set up a governance process, picked some KPIs, trained some analysts, and shown everyone how to access data. Now let's move on to the next problem," goes the mantra of organizations that might have briefly scaled the top of Mount Enterprise before landing back at the Departmental Level. Instead, the thinking should be: "Let's continue to stay focused on this process to ensure all our efforts toward organizational transformation aren't for naught."

But even before organizations reach the backsliding phase, they often get stranded at the point where data-driven decision making hasn't quite seeped into the staff's collective bloodstream. Say you work at a hospital that has made dramatic strides in enterprise-wide information gathering, including building dashboards that measure hospital infection rates in nuanced detail—unit, floor, and date. Instead of a nurse manager getting a report quarterly or monthly, the information is refreshed daily and available to the nursing staff. Except the staff doesn't use the dashboard. They've gone through the class on how to read it and why it is important, and what to do when infections start popping up, but it isn't ingrained in their work flow. They figure if there is a problem someone from infection control will deal with it. Or perhaps the staff stares at a screen showing that the three patients released last week were readmitted with infections, but they don't troubleshoot because they've got too much else to do right now. The institution taught the nursing staff how to use the information, it empowered them to troubleshoot the situation, it may even be dunning units with poor infection controls marks, but it didn't really change the culture if the staff doesn't have time to deal with what they're seeing or figures that it is someone else's problem to solve. This gets back to the alignment issue that is so critical. If people, processes, technology, or culture is out of alignment, the organization can't move forward.

Another example of risk at the Enterprise Level is what happens when an organization can't act on the information it is now able to acquire. Having the necessary information is useless if it can't be acted on. For instance, if a retailer plans a marketing campaign around sweaters featuring a certain kind of wool, and then learns from its suppliers that those sweaters are going to cost a lot more because of conditions in the wool market, it must be able to rework the plans to focus on other products. If the company has the Enterprise Level view, but doesn't have the processes, skills, and infrastructure to support rapid redeployment, its Enterprise Level maturity isn't returning on its investment like it should.

CONTINUOUS IMPROVEMENT REQUIRED

Business units in Department Level organizations have a natural impetus to stay at the highest functioning end of that level—it makes them look good. In contrast, staying at the Enterprise Level requires constant vigilance. The Enterprise Level organization must make sure data governance and policies to control the accuracy and flow of enterprise information are followed by all business units on an ongoing basis. Keeping an eye on internal alignment between business units is also critical. Since all decision makers and business units in this type of organization have access to integrated enterprise information, their decision-making process is faster. As a result, there may be an increased sense of autonomy that should be monitored and managed to support the enterprise objectives. Executive sponsorship remains critical. If a Center of Excellence was formed to help the organization reach this level it should remain open for business with its charter modified to focus on continuing the progress toward a higher maturity level.

Achieving the Enterprise Level is no small accomplishment. This step eludes many organizations. But when it does happen, leadership quickly realizes the strategic advantages of continuing along the information evolution path. It shouldn't be a tough sell to start the discussion to move to the Optimized Level.

BUSINESS TRANSFORMATION STRATEGY OBJECTIVES FOR FOUNDATIONAL ORGANIZATIONS

If you believe your organization has achieved Enterprise Level maturity, then the really tough part is done. Your organization value chain is now clear and available to all decision makers. Your organization is at the tipping point to achieve higher levels of maturity and competitive advantage if it can put together a business transformation strategy to move to the Optimize and Innovate Levels. Your business transformation strategy should include the following objectives:

- Assess your current organization capabilities in the four key pillars to validate the maturity level on which your organization is operating and determine gaps in capabilities.

- Identify business areas that can benefit from optimizing their operation using enterprise information and insight from value chain information.

- Focus on identifying and acquiring the skills needed to optimize business operation.

 THE WORLD REALLY CAN BE SMALLER

Enterprise Level organizations are in a much better position to engage in the global market because they have developed a clearer understanding of their business model and value chain. Expanding the business to new markets requires comprehensive understanding of the organization's product cost, profitability, and marketability in new markets. Expansion may also require that the organization develop new skills and a partner network. Enterprise Level organizations have done the essential groundwork needed to understand the cost and profitability of their products and services. This information tends to be missing in action at the Challenged Level organizations.

CHAPTER **5**

Progressive Organizations: Harnessing the Power of Information to Achieve Market Advantage and Expand Their Business Offerings

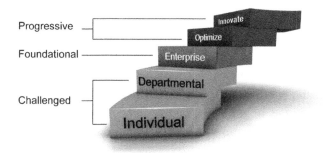

Wʜat we've learned so far: Moving to the Enterprise Level is a key step that provides a foundation for higher levels of maturity. Enterprise organizations are at a tipping point to achieve higher levels of competitive advantage by using their resources and talents to optimize and innovate. Reaching the Enterprise Level does require constant vigilance as it is easy for people, information processes, technology, and culture to slip out of alignment. Maintaining that alignment, and exploring the value that enterprise-wide information brings, is eye-opening.

In the fast-changing marketplace you need to move quickly and proactively to counter market forces. That's the reason to work toward the integrated enterprise-wide view of information emblematic of a Foundational Level organization. Is that enough? While having a clear picture of the value chain lowers your organization's risk, it doesn't take full advantage of the opportunities that come with integrated data. For this, organizations need to head for the Optimize and Innovate Levels.

Optimizing is about more than regularly using insight-driven decision making—as opposed to using it in an occasional project—it is about *automating* insight-driven decision making. The enterprise-wide view of data allows the organization to create a model that suggests the best price, the service plan most likely to entice a customer, or the defect (from warranty data) that manufacturing needs to address now. Optimized organizations use their understanding of their value chain to look for opportunities to drive the unnecessary cost out of their operations. They analyze their suppliers list and identify the ones that provide the best prices, relationship, and future potential for expanded partnerships. They analyze their interactions with customers, identify the most profitable ones, and develop strategies to keep their elite customers loyal and engaged. They take the same approach with their products and services to identify the profitable ones on which to focus as well as the not-so-profitable ones and subject them to critical analysis to determine their fate. They look for best practices and innovative methods to improve and align their internal functions. What do they get in return? Tangible improvement in their performance and market position and increased alignment with their suppliers and partners.

There is another key factor at play here: Optimized organizations do all this in ways that are highly automated and embedded in the process. It is not a one-time project to discover the most profitable customers; it is an ongoing process.

Often the narrative on innovative organizations suggests gutsy risk-taking ventures, the flouting of conventional wisdom, and bold, visionary leadership. The last part is correct in the sense that organizations at the Innovative Level typically require visionary leadership to drive information maturity to the point where it can support innovation. A good idea, after all, is just the beginning. Before that comes an exceptional understanding of the value chain, such that the organization can quickly and easily model new products or services. These organizations leave observers thinking not only "Why didn't we think of this?" but "How did they know that would be so successful?"

Innovative Level organizations think this way: "With the talent and knowledge we have, why should we limit ourselves to a specific line of product or industry?" That is when the executive vision, combined with innovative talent in the workforce, enables organizations to think about new products and services. These organizations institute a process and a culture that encourages and rewards prototyping new products and services. They use their own information as well as all possible external market information to study consumer behavior and the available products in the market, and look for opportunities they can capitalize on.

For both of these Progressive Levels, fact-based decision making is the norm. These organizations have put in the tough work of identifying enterprise-wide KPIs and have the flexibility to know when and how to change them up. Gut instinct has left the building. It's not coming back.

OPTIMIZATION: THE EASIEST BUSINESS CASE OF ALL

Optimization is the brass ring that analytics has been promising organizations for at least the past decade. But in a siloed environment, failures and stalled progress are likely. Retailers have embraced markdown optimization to move merchandise quickly—get rid of the bathing suits in August and holiday ornaments in January. But if the data isn't being fed back to vendors, planners, and assortment packers, the value of optimization is muted.

One international retail organization has deployed optimization better than most by reducing its involvement in the daily decision making involved in restocking goods. It opened up its internal store ordering systems to suppliers so they can see which stores need a fresh shipment of diapers or a dozen cases of apple juice. The organization incorporated weather forecast information that predicts severe weather, and used their supply chain to ship storm items to their stores in the affected areas. They carefully established all the business, engagement, and pricing rules to govern their relationships with their suppliers. Then, instead of getting mired in the tactical issues of diaper dispersal, headquarters works on the strategic issues—finding and pairing with suppliers that will provide the best price and service.

Optimization is transformative. A national shoe retailer wanted to eliminate the problem of Store A selling out of a certain size or style rapidly while Store B was heavily marking down the same style and size. It began analyzing store sales to find patterns that could suggest better assortment packs. Retailers have done this in the past in an ad hoc, "gut" sort of way. Boston got more boots and Miami got more flip flops. But this retailer, working in a well-integrated data environment, analyzed at a much more granular level using both past sales data and customer "frequent shopper" information. It doesn't just know that boots sell in Boston; it knows which Boston stores have a lot of size-8 customers who like edgier fashions. Stockouts have dropped, margins have improved, markdowns are fewer, and vendors have now bought into the process.

The optimized organization now has the ability to monitor the marketplace and quickly realign itself to meet market demands. It can incrementally improve the profit margin by removing cost from the process wherever possible. Both approaches improve the ability to compete. If you can do optimization better than anyone else in your market, you will achieve sustainable market leadership and competitive advantage.

The progression from the Enterprise Level to the Optimized Level is fluid because it requires no significant overhaul on any dimension, just incremental enhancements in each supported by sound executive leadership. However, this level represents the point at which organizational focus must shift from collecting and integrating data to using the value chain for optimization in every facet of the organization. These organizations will need new talents who understand how to optimize the organization value chain. That is how gaining genuine value from that data is realized. Paramount to success is consistent executive direction.

 WHAT THE OPTIMIZED LEVEL ORGANIZATION LOOKS LIKE

■ The organization optimizes every business function by driving the cost out and maximizing profit. It becomes more in touch with external market conditions and can foresee the slightest shift in expectations.

■ It increases appetite for more data than ever because the organization monitors and analyzes structured and unstructured data from many sources: markets, customers, partners, suppliers, social networks, blogs, and wikis.

■ It expands global operations as better data controls make these ventures less risky and more profitable.

Along with better partner and supplier collaboration, Optimized Level organizations have mastered the data quality and governance issues that lower information maturity organizations struggle with. The infrastructure is more open to integrating external data and contact channels to improve insight. The metadata model documents the entire business process, value, and strategy. Everything is transparent. A closed-loop infrastructure feeds results back into the system to create a continuous learning environment.

Self-Managing Knowledge Workers

The Optimized Level organization has fewer worker bees and more knowledge workers tasked with using analytics for strategy and performance management. These employees are typically given wide-spanning authority. The command and control management style is phased out. Collaborative work  is valued, and there is emphasis on incremental process improvement.

Finding and retaining the right workers can be challenging, as the people who thrive in this environment are in great demand. In addition, some of the skills that help an organization get to the Enterprise Level may now be redirected to focus on optimization. It is essential to identify the employees who showed the greatest flexibility and drive at earlier levels and provide them the training and resources necessary to succeed at the Optimized Level. One organic way to identify the high flyers is through peer groups that are now formalized across departments. These groups get together for brainstorming sessions on how to identify and allocate cost to the various functions and processes in the organization value chain. Employees and decision makers leverage information and use trending, pattern analysis, forecasting, and predictive analytics to increase effectiveness, profitability, and quality, which leads to incremental improvement in market share and competitive advantage.

Reaching this level is disruptive. Resource realignment and the continuous skill-improvement requirement can leave employees wondering how they fit into the organization. Change management and training programs are critical to maintaining this level. The employees who acted as a conduit between the organization and vendors, those tasked with marking down merchandise, anyone who had specific skills and relationships, naturally fear they will become obsolete. While executives see optimization as a way to free resources for more, the resources are worried about job security. It becomes even more important that the right training and reward systems are in place. Those who think outside the box to achieve greater optimization deserve additional training, new opportunities, and advancement.

OPTIMIZED LEVEL: PEOPLE

- The staff is focused on incremental process improvement.
- Autonomy and empowerment are common.
- Cross-business unit peer groups become established.
- Knowledge workers are prized, rewarded, and given adequate training.

Feeding the Continuous Improvement Loop

Self-improvement is paramount at this level. Information processes established at the Enterprise Level are now expanded to provide feedback that drives optimization of internal and external functions. Best practices are captured to replicate successes and to prevent repeated mistakes.

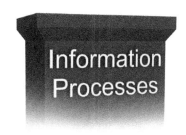

Project experience is documented, and new project teams start by checking out these corporate experiences. New projects are designed to evolve into ongoing, automated processes.

In order to optimize, these organizations put in place new information processes that govern how external information sources are integrated with organizational data. They ask vendors and suppliers to participate in the information sharing process and optimization efforts. This collaboration helps strengthen relationships with suppliers and partners and provides the organization with a better understanding of their partners' knowledge, capabilities, and potential.

Many optimization efforts, though, give customers the sense that they're working with a forward-looking organization. Let's look at a financial institution that wants to boost its credit card business. The local megamall is hosting a big promotion. If the bank can automate a text message about the promotion to customers near the mall, and offer five percent cash back, it magnifies the impact of the pitch. It's not just a message about five percent cash back or just a message about a mall promotion. It shows the bank's attempt to understand the consumer's shopping preferences and desire to provide relevant value in the form of cash back for purchases the consumer is buying anyway.

Plus, business units have a strong set of processes and tools to better analyze whether these kinds of efforts yield a strong enough return on investment. Discoveries in one unit can be quickly applied across the organization. For example, if combining two items on a promotional web page doubled sales of the cross-sell item, that knowledge can be rapidly exported to in-store displays.

As the organization learns more about the value chain, the metrics evolve to emphasize a more outward focus. Measures are defined and tracked across time periods for the entire business value chain. These might include employee productivity, sales growth rate, customer satisfaction, time to market, and adoption rate of new products and customers. Cause-and-effect relationships among performance metrics get closer scrutiny. The global restaurant company that learned that quick service wasn't enough was able to find the "sweet spot" where fresher taste didn't take so long that customers complained about the wait. This is also often the point at which organizations discover that seemingly sound business or marketing practices are counterproductive—such as when a telecommunications provider learns that the customers with the highest-priced plans are not always the most profitable.

OPTIMIZED LEVEL: INFORMATION PROCESSES

- Best practices are captured to replicate successes and prevent repeated mistakes.
- KPIs are tweaked to better understand root causes and drive performance.

- Information is pulled in from outside sources.
- The organization works collaboratively with vendors and suppliers.
- Functions for outsourcing are easily identified.

Anywhere, Anytime Intelligence

Optimized Level organizations accelerate their adoption of new technologies and concepts, especially those that strengthen the relationship with customers, partners, and suppliers. They use the insight they develop from understanding their value chain, and develop multiple cross-function business performance views to enable them to analyze their value chain and look for business, process, and product optimization opportunities. Multiple data marts that integrate products, customers, and channel information are developed. Various views of customer satisfaction, microsegmentations, and customer value analysis are used to enhance customer experience and validate business assumptions of product quality and value. The goal is to be well-positioned to derive the most insight from social media, along with knowing when cloud computing, software as a service, and high-performance analytics can make a difference. They are eager to adopt technologies that help them understand the broader aspects of their customers' behavior using social media analytics and manage risk in real time using high performance analytics. They are very focused on driving incremental improvements, and can easily and quickly build the business case to strengthen their information infrastructure capabilities.

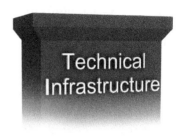

The Optimized Level organization has a highly calibrated sense of the analytic functions that need to remain centralized and those that should be pushed down to the business unit. Because the data is well governed, these organizations can keep specialized high-end analytic activities embedded in the business unit, knowing the results of those efforts aren't at odds with enterprise-wide insight. While information integration suggests centralized control, decision makers in business units can actually have more autonomy and flexibility.

 FAILURE IS OKAY

In organizations at this level, failure is part of the learning process as they start to look at what customer behavior signs or events might indicate the customer is leaving—or which marketing messages and channels are more effective to attract a certain age group or demographic. These are difficult questions to answer. Using analytics to figure out answers to these business challenges requires the exploration of various alternatives and hypotheses. Exploring the validity of some of the options may not produce positive outcomes. These practices are viewed as constructive steps in the learning process and are accepted as necessary to arrive at the correct outcome. The organization is so agile that missteps can be easily foreseen or overcome—and prevented from recurring. This supportive attitude works both ways. People are willing to accept the concept of compromise for the good of the organization if they know the organization is willing to compromise for them.

The use of technology goes far beyond the classic business intelligence drill, sort, filter, and rank—the calculations and tallies that are sometimes mistaken for analytics. At this level, organizations use analytics to predict future outcomes of interest; explore and understand complex relationships in data; and model customer behaviors and processes. Business analytics tools model workflow interactions to develop new and improved business processes. They monitor cause-and-effect relationships to continue finding opportunities to improve. They examine customer information to detect patterns that predict future behavior. And they get answers in real time, or close to it. Knowledge workers can forecast and predict, not merely look at what happened in the past.

OPTIMIZED LEVEL: TECHNICAL INFRASTRUCTURE

- New technologies are adopted with comparative ease and better results.
- Function, process, and infrastructure de-duplication continue, saving time and money.
- Technology supports optimization, predictive analytics, and forecasting.
- Business units have access to high-quality enterprise information and high-end tools because the data is centralized, not the analysis of it.

Thriving on Change

At this level, change is a core competency—not a threat. The compensation system is structured around business performance (as measured by KPIs). The organization expects employees to apply critical thinking, validate assumptions, and determine root causes as bases for decisions. With  an adaptive information architecture, job descriptions, accountabilities, organizational structure, workflow, and processes are more fluid. This is important as change is rapid, iterative, and continuous—just as it is in the markets the organization serves.

Optimized Level organizations can't function unless collaboration is embedded in the culture. The environment promotes widespread sharing of internal and external information across business units and functions, providing a broad context for communities of interest to share their experiences and fine-tune the business. This culture of community now extends outside the organization to include customers, suppliers, and partners. Strategic thinkers are prized as visionaries, and their ideas are given a chance to fly. Some of these ideas will flop, but mistakes are not punished; they are viewed as learning experiences.

To tackle difficult business problems, these organizations form diverse teams, combining expertise from various business functions in ways they've never done before. Critical analytical, business, as well as technical skills are used to focus on optimizing the enterprise value chain, with information on the value chain documented and distributed to all business units and decision makers. Centers of Excellence play a key role. The centers help business units learn how to use data and analytics to answer questions like: "How can we identify cost imbedded in our processes?" "How can we identify the most profitable products and customers?" "How can we optimize our distribution routes?" "Will this process improvement be worth it?"

 OPTIMIZED LEVEL: CULTURE

Flexibility and adaptability are important traits.

- ▥ Employees are rewarded based on business performance.
- ▥ Collaboration is essential and ongoing.
- ▥ Analytics supports novel initiatives.
- ▥ Executive support remains constant.

Getting the Most from Optimization

The Optimized Level has challenges. It can sometimes be a struggle to win over vendors and suppliers to the "optimized" way of doing business—sharing performance and operational results. Optimization models can also be so complex that they take too long to run using conventional computing, such as a markdown optimization model that takes a day or more to run. Procuring cutting-edge, high-performance analytic technologies is necessary. There also needs to be a dedicated effort to care and feed information to the models that support optimization. At this level, modeling and advanced analytics are neither one-time projects nor a process that is set up to run into infinity. Models will change, competitive pressures shift, new sources of information emerge. The organization has to have the people, processes, technology, and culture to account for these issues and make changes as necessary.

Internal perception is another challenge. Because optimization introduces changes to the operating model, the organization needs to explain how it uses insight to optimize its value chain and to make decisions. Helping everyone understand the value of insight-driven decision making is paramount. This is particularly important in organizations that will continue to depend on a large pool of customer-facing staff (such as retailers, government entities, and telecommunication and hospitality providers). If the hotel desk clerk, the call center operator, or the assistant store manager doesn't understand why certain offers are being made—or doesn't trust the optimization's recommendations, seeking to override or ignore them—then efforts are jeopardized. Business performance dashboards for frontline staff can help.

Finally, even a good thing can be taken to an extreme. Optimization in and of itself can only wring out so much profit. And organizations may be at risk if they rest too much on their laurels and become too confident of their ability to control and protect their market share and success. In this global economy, continuing success will depend on innovation—and exploring different ways to improve performance, products, and services, and their understanding of their customers.

TOWARD INNOVATION AND BEYOND

Twenty years ago, you bought music on a compact disc, books came bound, and photos had to be developed. Toys were purchased at a store, and you needed to set a VCR to record a television show. Obviously things have changed. In many cases, the manufacturers of now rarely used products have changed. Others went out of business. Even in organizations that  were first to market with an innovative new product (think of the early smartphone producers) someone else comes along and does it better. All the more reason to try and reach for the Innovate Level.

As beneficial as it is to optimize your organization it can produce a sense of contentment, which leads to acceptance of the status quo, which may present a significant risk to organizations in industries undergoing rapid transformation. In other words: You can't rest on your laurels. Innovation—in terms of new products, new services, and new ways to deliver goods to your customers—is critical. Innovation, though, starts with a focus on what the enterprise does well—its core competencies. Having used insight to optimize the bottom line, organizations at this level are ready to use insight to focus on the top line.

A great example of this is health care plan organizations that have integrated their data to streamline their marketing campaigns, root out fraud, and provide competitive disease management programs. What's the next step? For some very sophisticated plans, teaming with pharmaceutical companies to conduct aftermarket studies on drugs and interactions is a logical step. After all, the health plan has a rich data source to tap—and skill in using it.

Or, take the example of a company that initially mastered selling books online. Then it figured out how to sell lots of other things on the web (sometimes in partnership and sometimes directly), then it looked at the struggling e-reader market and came out with its own version. Now it's helping authors bypass publishers. It wasn't the first company to sell products online or the first to develop an e-reader, and self-publishing has been around forever. This organization just kept building on its core competencies. Given the organization's success, it's a sure bet that data isn't siloed and analytics is well practiced.

WHAT THE INNOVATE LEVEL ORGANIZATION LOOKS LIKE

- Proactive and continuous innovation
- Fosters and rewards innovation
- Exceptional at incorporating outside data sources
- Analytics-driven product and service decisions differentiation
- Dominates industry and competes as a leader in a global market

The Innovate Level organization extends the value of previous maturity stages. This organization spawns new ideas and institutionalizes innovation. And it understands what it does well and applies this expertise to new areas of opportunity. There seem to be no limits to the new ideas that employees put forth, ideas that bring revenue from new sources. Some of the most inventive ideas are gleaned from other industries and unlikely inspirations.

Everyone in the organization is encouraged to offer up new ideas through a well-established process. New ideas are routinely modeled and prototyped to identify the ones that have the merit and potential to drive the organization forward. Groups with various competencies are formed to analyze and prototype new products and services. Go/ no-go decisions are based on information and sophisticated descriptive and predictive analytics that include data from the entire value chain—from sources inside and outside the organization. A principal focus is innovation that is driven by a well-defined internal process that encourages prototyping, piloting, and exploration in new markets. These organizations dominate their industry in market share, taking bold risks, setting new trends, and breaking new ground. Their efforts are based on a thorough understanding of their customers' behaviors, market changes, and product values. Their innovative approach puts them ahead of their competitors.

Creative Collaborators

In addition to the people needed to run and optimize the business, the organization attracts and rewards individuals who can synthesize information and ideas from multiple industries and interpret these to propose new and viable services and products. People  are expected to think like entrepreneurs. Hungry ones. These people are hard to find, but the organization has made an ongoing commitment to hire and retain them in part by providing a stimulating environment for creative thinkers who like to challenge old paradigms and work outside the box. In many cases, organizations can also identify existing human resources who have intimate knowledge of the organization value chain and capabilities as well as the creative and innovative minds. In this dynamic environment, anyone in the organization can bring a new idea to the table. The toughest aspect for these organizations? Identifying and encouraging this creative process, and keeping the critical resources engaged. Losing this talent will significantly hinder this innovative process.

It is also important to recognize that these skills are not just product, marketing, or analytical resources. They include executives and leaders who create the environment and culture to foster innovation. Think of Steve Jobs's career and involvement in Microsoft before leading Apple. His vision and creativity made him an icon in the industry and propelled Apple, from a performance and consumer perspective, to a leader and trendsetter as it broke new ground in many areas of telecommunications and media. Its success was clearly based on its ability to better and earlier understand consumers' preferences and requirements. It took bold risks in creating new product interfaces and in creating the worldwide collaboration of partners that contributed to its success by developing products that work on its iPhone and iPad products. It managed to get thousands of organizations to indirectly promote its products.

People at the Innovate Level truly represent a cross-section of different talent types—from efficiency experts to right-brain-centered individuals. Multidisciplinary skills are common. Differences in background, experience, and knowledge are embraced and encouraged. Collaboration is all the richer when the participants bring unique perspectives to the table. Cross-functional peer groups continue to play a key role in an individual's day. Peer groups are always looking to broaden the diversity of the team—all the better for the most vibrant brainstorming sessions and the most creative ideas.

INNOVATE LEVEL: PEOPLE

- Individuals with varied skill sets are cultivated.
- Collaboration is expected.
- Creativity is prized.
- Entrepreneurial personalities fit well.

Managing Constant Renewal

There is no rest for the process guardians at the Innovate Level organization. In addition to keeping the well-defined processes built up over time, these organizations need new processes and policies for managing innovation. A project incubation process is used to grow new ideas and move them quickly into prototype and pilot stages. The results of innovation are routinely managed, evaluated, and communicated in a well-structured manner. The innovation pipeline is analyzed just like a portfolio of risk. The Innovate Level organization stays on top of issues such as technology readiness, barriers to market entry, the impact of a new project on existing processes, and—more important—on its existing customer base.

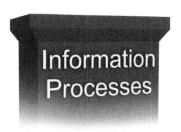

New metrics reflect the importance of innovation, such as revenue from new ventures, number of ideas at various stages of the development process, time from idea to launch, and the projected value of new ideas in the pipeline.

 INNOVATE LEVEL: INFORMATION PROCESSES

- Business processes are self-learning and self-tuning.
- Process to prototype and pilot new products and services is well-defined.
- Performance metrics reflect the importance of innovation.
- Comprehensive and mature governance processes and policies continue to evolve.

Growing a Support Network for Innovation

The integrated, enterprise-wide IT architecture continues to update and distribute value chain information to all decision makers and support the optimization process with appropriate data marts that provide integrated information from various business functions. The exploration of new ideas that may produce new products or services requires additional integration and consolidation of internal and external information. Innovate Level organizations dedicate technical resources to support this critical need. Teams with appropriate technical, analytical, and domain resources are

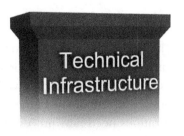

quickly formed to support timely analysis and exploration of new prototypes that have been approved in a laboratory-type environment. The infrastructure becomes an information hub to support creativity, with options for sharing, reviewing, commenting, and analyzing information. It includes a kind of content management system for assembling internal and external information needed to spawn new ideas, manage the pipeline of new ideas, and move along ideas deemed worthy to pursue. The infrastructure accepts structured and unstructured data in a variety of media, such as databases, text documents, graphics, e-mail, and digitized voice communications. Proposals and pilot projects are documented and categorized and are easily accessible for reference and use. Post-pilot reviews are documented and made available for learning.

Predictive analytics is used extensively to model the future—to identify potential ideas quickly, rule them out or approve them, and minimize the risk of moving forward with any of them. "What if" becomes a daily question, and analytics provides reliable answers based on quality information. Risk management systems and human capital management systems take on new life.

Information access is generally widespread among knowledge workers, but when sensitive information is needed to speed research and prototyping efforts it is done quickly with an established protocol that recognizes the importance of speed to market. The organization's information infrastructure is adaptable enough to provide a secure environment or laboratory to support innovation.

 INNOVATE LEVEL: TECHNOLOGY INFRASTRUCTURE

▪ Allows rapid analysis of new business and marketing opportunities.

- Affords knowledge workers easy access to information—with appropriate security measures for protecting intellectual property.
- Supports analysis of many different types of internal and external data, including unstructured data.
- Incorporates a broad variety of information delivery and analysis options.

A Culture of Entrepreneurial Innovation

One of the chief reasons organizations need to become insight-driven is to replace gut instinct and intuition. In disorganized, data-immature organizations intuition is problematic, as it is too often used to justify wrong decisions. At the Innovate Level, intuition gets a seat at the table again, but with  a twist. This is because the culture is aligned so that creative individuals draw on their instincts—and on data—to make decisions and explore new products and services. These are organizations that are successful enough to avoid failures, because they've learned how to efficiently vet ideas and pull the plug before large costs have been accrued. After all, perhaps only one idea in ten will be funded for further development and one in one hundred of those actually brought to market. But if the idea can be quickly brought from concept to fruition the discarded ideas don't impact the bottom line like they might in an organization that doesn't have the insight and maturity to rapidly model them in a virtual environment and track the pipeline just like it manages tangible products.

Innovate Level organizations function like magnets drawing in highly skilled, creative workers—although finding those who fit the culture can be a challenge. And helping existing employees stay up to date on the organizational evolution requires a sophisticated internal communications team. In addition, the organization must balance the types of knowledge workers it employs. Some highly skilled, highly creative individuals prefer to work as "lone wolves," which can cause friction at an organization that needs to form and reform teams to better innovate. Innovate organizations are always working to strike the right balance.

Innovate Level organizations don't fear market volatility; they meet it head-on through continuous innovation. These organizations deliver a constant stream of new products, services, and business models—staying ahead of the competition to sustain market leadership. When competition or commoditization threatens one source of revenue, the organization had already predicted and considered this outcome, and is already prepared to release the next product.

As is the case in other levels of maturity, these organizations face the risk of losing focus. Daily tactical and operational responsibilities still exist—and finding the right mix of staff to monitor the more routine activities is needed. The challenge is to constantly hone the business strategy, being careful not to stray too far away from core competencies or stray too far out of alignment with market conditions and customer demands.

INNOVATE LEVEL: CULTURE

- New ideas are continuously evaluated.
- Permission to fail is considered part of the creative and innovative process.
- A proactive approach to information and market research protects the organization when competition or commoditization threatens one source of revenue.
- Executive leadership supports an entrepreneurial approach to innovation.

Stopping at the Optimized Level—Or Striving toward the Innovate Level

"At what level do we really need to be?" Given the information maturity level most organizations are at, the question seems simple. Organizations absolutely must break out of the Individual and Departmental mind-set and progress toward an enterprise-wide approach. The Enterprise Level is without question the starting point and the foundation to gain the efficiencies of the Optimized Level and the competitive and proactive advantages of the Innovate Level. Enterprise Level should be the minimum level of organizational maturity. Many factors will influence the strategy to move forward toward the higher level. These factors include the organization's size and global reach, the industry and the market competitive pressure, and the history and legacy of the organization. There are good reasons to always work on optimizing the organization's value chain to drive out unnecessary cost. And there are also many cases where innovation to expand the current portfolio of products and services is necessary for survival in today's very competitive global market. And, finally, it is important to also point out that once organizations achieve a reasonable level of value chain optimization, they may assign various priority levels to drive innovation in their different business functions.

BUSINESS TRANSFORMATION STRATEGY OBJECTIVES FOR PROGRESSIVE ORGANIZATIONS

Your organization is in much better shape compared to the majority of organizations if you believe you have achieved some of the capabilities and characteristics of the Optimized and the Innovate organizations. Chances are that these progressive improvements may not be widespread across the organization's business units, or your organization is at the early stages of this maturity journey. To continue to progress and not lose momentum, many organizations at this stage have the following objectives for their business transformation strategy:

- Assess your current organizational capabilities in the four key pillars and determine business priorities and gaps in capabilities.
- Focus on evaluating the current resources in critical areas to ensure the appropriate talents are acquired and retained.
- Focus on internal communication, change management, and training to support the desired innovative and progressive culture.

What Is Next after Finding Your Current Organization Maturity Level

This chapter, as well as Chapters 3 and 4, has provided descriptions to help you figure out at what level your organization is working currently, what levels are optimal, and some of the characteristics of each level with examples of what organizations can accomplish (or can't) at the various information maturity levels. In the following chapters, you will read about the role of a Center of Excellence at each maturity stage, with some examples of organizations that have successfully moved to a more mature level and a roadmap to help your organization get started.

CHAPTER 6

Centers of Excellence: The Key to Accelerate Organizational Transformation

What we have learned so far: As organizations move through each level they increase their opportunities to drive down costs, increase revenue, and improve the bottom line. However, evolving into a more insight-driven organization takes a lot of work. Reshaping the culture is critical, establishing uniform information processes is necessary, developing a strong skilled staff is equally important, and acquiring and properly using technology to develop an effective information infrastructure is vital. The past chapters have mentioned the role of a Center of Excellence (CoE) in helping organizations mature. Some organizations also use the term Business Intelligence Competency Center (BICC). This chapter explores that concept.

The biggest issue organizations confront when they decide to take their information and analytical maturity to a new level is how to go about it. It is a daunting task that can't be outsourced or bought. The best plan of attack should include the following steps:

Step 1: Secure executive-level sponsorship to lead and support the organization's effort not only initially but throughout the information maturity journey.

Step 2: Evaluate organizational maturity to determine capabilities, weaknesses, and gaps that may prevent the organization from achieving its business objectives.

Step 3: Develop a strategy that outlines how the organization will address gaps and develop the capabilities to achieve its business objectives.

Step 4: Determine what role the Center of Excellence will take and outline a structure, engagement processes, and needed skills.

Step 5: Produce a roadmap that breaks down the required steps into reasonable and manageable phases.

No two CoEs are exactly alike, just as no two organizations have the exact same issues or maturity level. Nor are CoEs silver bullets that can solve all problems. They can, however, play a significant role in leading the organization's effort throughout its journey to a higher maturity level, and in introducing efficiency and productivity measures and best practices that can eliminate duplication of effort and improve decision quality. These benefits are essential to the success of any information strategy.

CoEs aren't static entities. They evolve as the organization evolves and should take on different roles throughout the organization's maturity journey. They might have permanent staff, or people on loan. They might work in a central location, or operate as a virtual team. The structure for a CoE should meet the needs of the organization and take into account the internal culture.

When a bank decided it wanted to increase its informational and analytical maturity to improve its business performance it built a CoE that was focused on breaking down information silos that had been formed by business units. The first order of business was to make sure each business unit was represented in the CoE organization.

The bank recognized the required effort, and demonstrated its commitment to this critical initiative by establishing a permanent CoE organization dedicated to achieving this objective. The CoE was staffed with technical and banking domain experts and business intelligence and analytics staff. The goal was to improve the quality of information used for making decisions, and to enhance the information infrastructure to supply the right information at the right time, and in the right format, to decision makers. This insider/outsider approach worked perfectly for this organization. It saw substantial ROI gains from efforts to develop an enterprise-wide view of its customers and services.

A manufacturing company took a different approach. It created a CoE with the goal of routing all its high-end analytics projects through the CoE. It thought it would be a better use of resources to keep all the analytical exploration in one location. While the company has reported successes, it isn't doing much to make its internal analytics efforts more process focused. Instead, the CoE takes a very project-based mentality and has become a bottleneck. It is not doing an effective job of advancing the use of information throughout the organization. While it is an improvement on the previous method of pestering IT for information, all it has done is create another queue.

CoEs should be figuring out how to eliminate queues—not form them. Depending on an organization's maturity stage, a CoE might initially support analytical and BI requirements with the long-term objective of promoting self-service. It may also help eliminate data silos, bring together business units to discuss KPIs, or search out outstanding business unit analytic efforts to help other units benefit from those insights. At its heart, it moves the organization toward developing skills and processes that make fact-based and analytically driven decisions a part of the organization's DNA. This will require changing the organization's mentality regarding its information from a "project" approach to an ongoing "process" approach that is embedded in day-to-day activities. Successful organizations keep the following question foremost in their mission: "Are both data and analytics regarded and managed as strategic assets in our organization?"

WHAT'S IN A NAME?

A Center of Excellence doesn't need to be called that. What's important is to consider the message it sends the organization. Avoid using a name that suggests a limited scope. For instance, using the name "Business Intelligence CoE" suggests the center will focus solely on querying and reporting. In some instances, the implementation roadmap will limit the CoE's focus to support a specific business function, yet choosing a broader name will help you avoid renaming the center as you move through the maturity levels. One idea: Call it the Enterprise Business Analytics CoE. "Business analytics" encompasses all areas of information management, including data integration, BI, analytics, performance management, and the various solutions that support business functions. Using this term provides the organization with the flexibility to expand and change the focus of the CoE as it moves through the maturity journey. Including the term "CoE" in the name is not critical.

THE 10,000-FOOT VIEW OF INFORMATION

CoEs are assigned the critical role of providing the proverbial big picture view, seeing the good and the bad. One of the main lessons Dan Ariely gleaned from the research for his book *Predictably Irrational: The Hidden Forces That Shape Our Decisions* is that "although irrationality is commonplace . . . once we understand when and where we make erroneous decisions, we can try to be more vigilant, force ourselves to think differently about these decisions or use technology to overcome our current shortcomings."[1] Just as individuals have unique interpretations, biases, and cognitive blind spots, so do organizations. They often struggle to understand how mature they are in information usage and what they need to get to the next level. CoEs help organizations see where those erroneous decisions are coming from, why business units have different interpretations of the enterprise business performance, and what can be done to fix these problems. They are sort of like an on-site think tank, asking questions such as, "Are we sharing results effectively across the organization?" A CoE should be the group that can challenge "business as usual" and, most important, sponsor continuous learning and improvement. A CoE should also encourage business leaders to explore different ways to analyze their information and make decisions. The very nature of this exploration process will lead to unsuccessful attempts and false starts. Exploring the different options is a healthy practice that will ultimately lead to the best approach. Executive sponsors must grant "permission to fail" in order to help the CoE succeed.

Another key CoE role is as the "Cultural Driver" and "Change Agent" that removes the blinders, empowers the right people, and creates the information process framework that helps organizations reach the enterprise level—and beyond. Although the CoE can be virtual or permanent, it should ideally have the following characteristics:

- Supported and sponsored by executive-level management
- Funded and staffed by the organization
- Staffed by business, domain, analytical, and IT experts
- Established with well-defined focus, roles, responsibilities, and processes

A QUICK LOOK AT THE KEY RESPONSIBILITIES OF A CoE

Regardless of what drives an organization to establish a CoE, its charter should be well-defined. It needs to be able to work with any and all stakeholders, from IT and the teams responsible for collecting and storing data to the business units who use data to make decisions such as how to market products and from whom to buy supplies. A significant portion of its charter should be committed to understanding the information flow throughout the organization and improving this process so that all decision makers have valid and consistent information. This will require a close collaboration with the IT team that manages the information environment (including a data warehouse and marts). The CoE should become the link that connects business requirements to the information sources, understanding both the supply of available information and the demand for it. In many organizations, that link is not well established. Many information sources may exist that contain inconsistent and duplicate information. These are the dreaded silos that have been developed over time. Although the silos were meant to support the business, the inconsistent information embedded in them becomes one of the root causes of different interpretations of business performance. Maintaining these silos comes at a high cost in terms of duplication of data and efforts. A CoE can lead the effort to de-silo the organization, introducing efficiency, eliminating duplication, and documenting the information flow across the organization. Ultimately, a CoE helps the business identify the right source for information. If the required information is not available, or if it is available in multiple locations, the CoE will lead the effort to identify the proper information architecture.

The CoE keeps in mind that information sources need to:

- Support the business decision process and facilitate the production of business insight through the application of analytics and the use of effective performance management and business solutions.

- Be governed to ensure Master Data is managed properly and the IT architecture requirements are addressed to ensure a strong link between supply and demand.

- Be maintained by using best practices to create repeatable and efficient information acquisition and use, and to enable closed-loop learning to allow for continuous improvement.

MORE EXAMPLES OF CoE TEAM RESPONSIBILITIES

- Develop and promote information management and analytical best practices to facilitate the identification of analytical requirements, the application of analytics, and the interpretation and distribution of results.
- Educate the organization on the importance of data quality and support or lead the effort to manage master data.
- Help the decision makers develop analytics and information competency to support and guide fact-based and timely decisions.
- Leverage available analytical skills and resources to optimize their contribution to priority projects and business requirements.

- Gradually change the culture of the organization to always apply critical thinking and demand the validation of business assumptions and strategy.
- Foster a learning culture that encourages experimentation and provides permission to fail.
- Develop analytical talent and resources throughout the organization.

CoEs AND THE LEVELS OF MATURITY

The nature, structure, and role of the CoE will be different for organizations at different levels of maturity. At the Individual Level, information is not viewed as a valuable asset so there really is no point to having a CoE.

For organizations at the Departmental Level, it is possible to have business unit or departmental CoEs. These efforts might not be as organized as they should be in a true CoE, but they could provide the benefit of helping departments begin to do a better job of organizing information internally. But they can only be temporary structures because, as discussed earlier in the book, Departmental Level organizations are prone to developing information silos—and information silos are anathema to becoming an insight-driven organization. View the departmental CoE only as a stepping-stone to the eventual goal of having one consistent information architecture to serve the enterprise. Do not let these departmental CoEs become bulwarks of the political and cultural resistance to enterprise-level information sharing.

CoEs can provide a significant value in helping organizations reach the Enterprise Level. Some organizations establish an enterprise CoE to specifically drive the organization to this maturity level. Other organizations will provide some of the services and benefits of a CoE in an informal or temporary fashion during the deconstruction of information silos and establishment of an enterprise information environment.

As the Optimize and the Innovate Levels are progressive maturity levels, Enterprise CoEs are likely to exist in many forms. Organizations that reach one of these levels must have addressed their information challenges. There are situations where the concept, services, and role of an enterprise CoE can be observed in an organization in some form without being recognized as a CoE organization. While these efforts are clearly beneficial, introducing the formal best practice structure of an enterprise CoE is still worthwhile. It's important to note that the focus of a CoE in an organization that operates at one of the progressive maturity levels will clearly be different than organizations at lower levels (foundational and challenged) of maturity. These CoEs have the benefits of a well-integrated enterprise information architecture that can now focus on how to leverage the clean and consistent enterprise information to further propel the organization to higher levels of competitive advantage in the market. The use of analytics to validate assumptions and strategies and predict customers' behavior and preferences are all examples of CoE focus areas at the progressive organization maturity levels.

HOW SHOULD CoEs BE ORGANIZED?

Although the CoE should include experts drawn from various disciplines throughout the organization, there is no standard and fixed structure. The appropriate structure should be based on the organization's business priorities and capabilities. Each organization has strengths and weaknesses in its ability to produce and use business insight. The CoE should be structured to address weaknesses, supplement strengths, and enable it to achieve its business objectives. The CoE members must represent business users, technical specialists, and domain experts—the people who use information insight and analytics to make decisions along with those who actually produce that insight and build the analytical models. The optimal structure is a permanent organization with well-defined roles and responsibilities and KPIs to measure their contribution and impact. The team should be visible in the organizational structure and accessible to all the business units it intends to serve. Some organizations may start with a virtual team that combines the relevant resources from various locations. Although this approach may be quick to set up, it does present challenges in commitment, focus, and work prioritization, and should be only used as a temporary step toward a permanent structure. If dual reports have to moonlight to get their CoE work done, the virtual CoE concept won't work.

 ## TRAITS OF THE MOST EFFECTIVE AND STRATEGIC IMPLEMENTATIONS OF A CoE

The most effective and strategic implementations of a CoE have these traits:

- Partnering with business stakeholders for ongoing success
- Continuous and effective executive sponsorship
- Sufficient prominence in the organizational hierarchy to have visibility and impact.

ACCELERATING MATURITY—NOT CREATING DEPENDENCY

There are two interpretations of how a CoE should be structured. One interpretation sees it as an organization that acts as a change agent; the other is to consider it a shared services organization. The difference is significant, and it comes down to how organizations view the purpose and role of the CoE organization. The change agent approach is to think of a CoE as an effective tool to:

- Address inefficiencies in the current information management and analytical practices in the organization.
- Help organizations make the necessary changes to improve each organizational pillar.
- Accelerate the organization's effort to evolve to a higher maturity level as part of the broader organization's transformation roadmap.

To achieve these objectives, the business users have to be actively involved, and the CoE has to have the right resources with the required skills to act as the agent of change. Visibility, business impact, and executive support will be essential requirements for the CoE to achieve these objectives.

The other interpretation of a CoE is as an IT shared service organization that offers some type of technical service such as reporting or analytical support. Although this approach may improve how the organization responds to business requests, it reinforces a barrier between the business users and the technologies, critical thinking, and information analysis process needed to improve decision making.

IT shared service organizations encourage business units to send information and analysis requests to queue up to the organization and wait to get the results back. A shared service organization works on a project basis, handling "requests" for information and analytics, and in some cases they charge for these projects. The second example in the opening of this chapter is a "shared service" model. This model does nothing to help the business units successfully work with data and analytics on their own. Inevitably, bottlenecks evolve, and the use of analytics and information insight becomes a "project" and an undesirable burden, not a core component of the decision-making process. Frustrated with the long lines that form to get a spot on the CoE schedule (or the price), business units start patching together their own solutions, working with whatever data they've got and using whatever talent they have.

 TWO INTERPRETATIONS OF HOW A CoE SHOULD BE STRUCTURED

There are two interpretations of how a CoE should be structured. One interpretation sees it as an organization that acts as a change agent, while the other is to consider it a shared services organization. The difference is significant, and it comes down to how organizations view the purpose and role of the CoE organization.

In comparison, well-functioning CoEs help business users learn to use information and develop business insight themselves—they don't do it for them. A critical requirement of a well-structured CoE is to aggressively work toward promoting self-service capabilities to enable the business users to do as much as they can on their own. The technologies available today are often designed with business users in mind.

In addition, in order to avoid being an ineffective budgetary sink-hole that does nothing to move the organization to a greater level of informational maturity, the CoE needs a close connection and integration with the various business units. At all costs the CoE should avoid being chartered *only* for projects. A project-only focus rarely allows these CoEs to identify the root cause of data issues such as data inconsistency, availability of master data, data quality, and integration. Consequently, they may not be able to make recommendations to address the root cause of these problems since it is not part of their project completion objectives. Actually, in some cases, IT shared service organizations, or outsourced services that perform similar functions, are measured by the volume of completed projects, which completely ignores the need to improve the information infrastructure, improve internal skills and process, and change the culture.

FINDING THE RIGHT SPOT IN THE ORG CHART

The CoE should be located in a high—and visible—spot in the org chart. It needs to be accessible to all internal stakeholders and customers. The leader of the CoE must report to an executive sponsor at the C level. Since CoEs will be making recommendations and changes to help business users make better fact-based decisions, they need the backing and support from the executive team.

MAPPING THE MINI-UNITS THAT A CoE MIGHT HOST

An effective structure for a CoE is developed only after evaluating the organization's business priorities and its capabilities to produce and use the required business insight to achieve these objectives. The assessment of current organizational pillars will reveal the organization's capabilities, weaknesses, and strengths. There is no standard structure for a CoE that will work in every environment and culture. However, there are basic information functions that provide essential information capabilities that must be evaluated. Figure 6.1 shows the basic functions that should be considered for a CoE.

Figure 6.1 illustrates enterprise CoE key functions, which correspond to key information management practices that exist in any

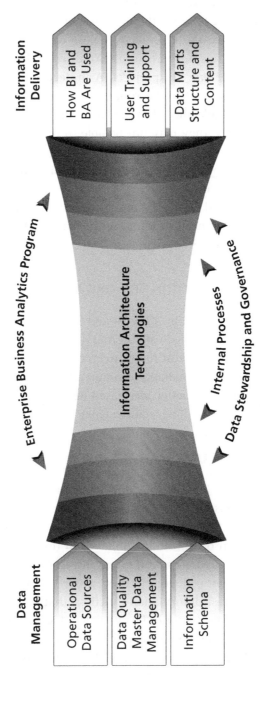

Figure 6.1 Key Functions of an Enterprise-Wide Center of Excellence

organization. As you can imagine, different levels of organizational maturities will have an impact on how well these areas are supported. Before we start exploring these key functions, keep in mind that a CoE may not have to address all of them. The assessment of the current organizational maturity and capabilities combined with a thorough gap analysis process will identify what type of a CoE is needed and which of these key functions should be addressed by the CoE. Let's start exploring these functions.

The information infrastructure of any organization brings operational and external data in, processes the data, and should produce good quality information to deliver it to the information consumers. We can think of this as a supply and demand environment. The process of taking raw data and converting it to useful enterprise information requires quite a bit of work, including the following key functions:

- Effective data integration
- Master data management
- Business intelligence capabilities to query and report on the data
- Application and effective use of analytics to produce business insight
- Application and use of performance management capabilities and principles
- Effective information management processes
- Data stewardship and information governance

This is the information value chain, and it is the heart of this discussion. When anyone talks about an organization's capabilities, it is in reference to this value chain. An enterprise CoE will carefully monitor this process to make sure it is functioning effectively. If one of these functions is working well, then we don't necessarily have to include it as a CoE function.

Data Management

This refers to the process of extracting operational systems data and external data and bringing it into the organization's information infrastructure. The infrastructure may include staging areas, data warehouses, and marts. To effectively manage this function you need a good understanding of the operational data sources, good management of the data quality, well-documented application of enterprise business rules, and master data management. All these functions and processes will load the extracted data into the organization's information infrastructure, which must have a well-defined information model or schema (usually a data warehouse model). The data management supplies information and makes it available to the information consumers.

Information Delivery

This key function represents the consumption of information by the business side. This is the demand side. Many of the inefficiencies and challenges in managing enterprise information may be attributed to the lack of alignment between supply and demand. Organizations will obviously need to produce the appropriate information that will satisfy the demand from a business consumer. To achieve this objective organizations, with the help from a CoE, will have to pay attention to how business requirements for information are managed and satisfied. How are the information consumers using business intelligence, analytics, or performance management? How well are the information marts structured to support the business users, and the skill levels of the business users? The information delivery function manages the demand side.

Enterprise Business Analytics Program

Information management practices need to be an ongoing process versus a series of projects that may not be well connected. The enterprise business analytics program function for the CoE addresses this very important requirement. This function will finally have an owner who is empowered to manage the key projects to stop redundancies, identify best practices, leverage skills, and so on. This critical function includes reaching out to all business, IT, and domain stakeholders to get them to collaborate and communicate more effectively. Depending on the unique requirements and maturity of each organization, this function may also include coordination with other business and IT initiatives involving master data or governance.

Data Stewardship and Governance

Wouldn't it be great if your enterprise information was always clean and consistent? That is not a very common attribute. In reality, enterprise data is often not high quality. To fix these challenges, you need to figure out the root causes and in doing so ask the questions: Who owns the data? Who owns the application systems? Who owns the data sources? These are the different areas in any organization that may impact data quality. Assigning an owner (steward) who is accountable for the data stored or managed by each one of these areas is needed to control the overall data quality flowing through the enterprise. There are potentially different types of stewards. A technical steward might work on data governance issues while a business steward could work on who has a right to access the information.

Ultimately, organizations will have to identify the different types of data stewards and the different data governance decisions and decision rights they will need to effectively manage enterprise information quality. Depending on the organization's maturity, a CoE team may be asked to play a role in addressing these critical functions.

Internal Information Processes

You have already explored several key information functions. To effectively perform each of these functions, individual processes need to be defined in order to help business units interact with each other, and engage with IT. Developing a comprehensive engagement model will facilitate the implementation of new recommendations. These processes are also essential to guide how business units and the IT team will interact with the CoE organization. The CoE may have to be involved in structuring and maintaining these processes. This is key to developing and maintaining effective information architecture.

HOW THE CoE HELPS SECURE THE ORGANIZATIONAL PILLARS

People, information processes, technology, and culture are this book's mantra for understanding how to evolve to a more mature organization. With that in mind it makes sense to also look at the organizational impact of a CoE from that perspective. Let's explore how a CoE can impact each of those pillars.

 KEY ROLE OF A CoE

One of the key roles of a CoE is to help the organization to evolve into a higher maturity level. This journey can only be successful when the four organizational pillars evolve together to a higher level of maturity.

Finding and Leveraging Talent

Good multidisciplinary resources are not easy to attract and retain. These leaders are usually driven by the desire to apply their knowledge to have a positive impact in their organization's business performance.

A Center of Excellence can:

- Leverage the specialized talents in various groups within the organization to get the most value of their contribution. This can be achieved by providing a method, process, and incentive for these talents to collaborate, share ideas, and develop best practices.

- Support the business units and the HR team in identifying the proper training, continuing education, and knowledge transfer for the critical talent across the organization.

- Raise awareness and support the organization's effort to develop meaningful job descriptions, job families, and an attractive career path to attract and retain critical talent.

Understanding and Communicating the Big Picture

Creating uniform, enterprise-wide information processes requires diplomacy and a detailed understanding of the needs of business units. It also requires careful analysis of the required information tasks to determine whether they are business or IT tasks. In addition, a careful and consistent analysis 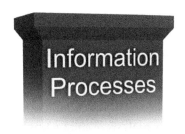 of these tasks and processes is essential for the organization to reach the right balance between centralizing and decentralizing these tasks. The CoE staff can look at the big picture, especially as it relates to the value chain, and communicate that information to decision makers, analysts, and other stakeholders. These business views should provide decision makers, analysts, and other stakeholders with a good understanding of the organizational value chain.

In addition, the CoE can:

- Be cognizant of industry best practices and apply them to current processes when appropriate.

- Carefully identify and analyze the required information processes to clearly define what should be handled and owned by the business and IT organizations.

- Recognize internal politics and identify obstacles and bring this knowledge to the executive sponsor with prescriptive recommendations to resolve these issues.

- Evaluate the current state of data quality, consistency, security, and access, and make recommendations.

- Establish processes to connect with data stewards in business areas to discuss and solve data quality issues and support the organization's data quality, master data, and governance initiatives.

- Develop processes to promote best practices around the use of analytics, performance management, and business solutions.

- Identify the best way for individuals to engage with the CoE and a process for working with other CoEs (if they exist).

Assessing the Impact of Technology

While technology often changes at a fast pace, people and organizational cultures don't. When figuring out whether a new technology is valuable you need to take a variety of issues into consideration, including the analysis of the technology impact on business users, culture and change

management requirements, resource requirements, and of course how this technology augments and integrates with other technologies and scheduled enhancements. The CoE is in a good position to help objectively assess the value of adopting technology improvements to meet the increasing business requirements and, more important, work with other IT and business groups to coordinate these enhancements with other initiatives planned for the organization.

A CoE can ask:

■ **Is the organization collecting and integrating enterprise information to support the decision-making process?** The ultimate test of the success of the organization's effort to manage its enterprise data is to answer yes to this question. One of the main objectives of establishing a CoE is to address the challenges organizations face when they try to integrate enterprise data and break the departmental silos. The CoE organization will have business user representatives to make sure business requirements are well defined. The CoE's job is to constantly manage the organization's information environment (data warehouses, marts, or any other architecture) to ensure the proper information is collected, integrated, and stored. Consequently, when executed properly, the concept of establishing an enterprise CoE will have a direct and visible impact on the organization's information infrastructure.

■ **Is there a business analytics strategy and architecture?** As business users continue to increase their use and reliance on BI, analytics, performance management, and business solutions, the process of coordinating these various efforts can be very inefficient.

A properly established CoE will own the requirement of developing and maintaining an enterprise business analytics strategy and architecture. This work must be done in close collaboration with the IT team to align the BA strategy and architecture with the enterprise IT information strategies and architectures.

▪ **What new technology should we use?** In addition, the CoE will be in the best position to evaluate and select new technologies to support the business requirements. In doing so, the CoE, in collaboration with the business users, will be evaluating the use of new technology to introduce efficiency and produce the insight to support the business decision-making process. The CoE can look into better ways to analyze information visually (using interactive and dynamic data visualization methods, exploring strategies and technologies to analyze big data, utilizing best practices for applying analytics in business solutions, and determining the pros and cons of using cloud-based or hosted options).

▪ **Does our strategy scale and extend to support the growing business requirements?** As the organization starts to organize its information management efforts, a long-term view of the extendability and scalability of the information architecture is necessary. The CoE will work closely with the IT team to ensure this requirement is met. This will allow the organization's information environment to keep up with the business requirements, manage the information infrastructure cost, and help justify the required investments in information infrastructure.

▪ **What types of analytic methods are needed?** Many low-maturity organizations get stuck in the rut of using regression analysis, or simple spreadsheet analysis. A CoE can work with the business users to identify the appropriate robust analytical methods to support the decision-making process, and ensure the information marts are properly structured to collect, store, and provide the right information in the right formation to support the required information analyses.

▪ **Are we using high-quality data to make decisions?** One of the critical requirements and benefits for the CoE is to support the organization's effort in cleaning its data, managing its master data, and applying the appropriate level of information governance. A properly executed CoE will support the organization's efforts around these topics and, depending on each environment, may take some or all responsibility to lead the organization's effort in these areas.

Communicating Value

The CoE can have one of its biggest impacts in the culture arena, helping set a tone that embraces fact-based and analytically driven decision making. This organization dimension is probably the hardest to change, but has the most significant impact on the organization's ability to become  insight-driven. Changing the organization's culture will take time, diplomacy, and careful changes to the way the organization evaluates its employees' performance, provides incentives and rewards, hires and promotes new skills, and communicates strategies and objectives. The CoE supports the organization's effort by communicating the organization's business priorities and objectives and demonstrating (through communicating its success stories) the value of business insight, analytics, and information as a corporate asset.

The CoE can:

- Work closely with the business users to demonstrate the value of using new technologies and support them in meeting their business objectives.

- Document and communicate new successes achieved by the business units using new methods, technology, and analytics.

- Work as a change agent to encourage business users to try new approaches and use new technologies to address their business priorities.

- Encourage experimenting with new ideas and accept unsuccessful attempts (from time to time) as part of the maturity process.

- Leverage existing domain and analytical skills to promote a collaborative atmosphere.

- Create an internal method to exchange ideas and re-use methods and techniques to solve business problems.

- Work closely with the heads of business units to dedicate resources and effort to support them in meeting their business objectives.

 ## PHASED VERSUS BIG BANG APPROACH FOR STARTING A CoE

Should you start in phases or go for a big commitment? A phased approach is more practical. Organizations generally learn a lot from the initial attempts to establish a CoE. Taking a phased approach enables them to use these lessons learned to evaluate and expand the scope of their CoEs through later iterations. It's important that a CoE establish credibility with early successes that build its reputation and earn it continual ongoing support from business units, IT, and executive sponsors. The phased approach should keep in mind an organization's level of maturity. An organization operating at the Departmental Level might inaugurate a CoE with the objective of breaking down the departmental silos. An Enterprise Level organization might use the CoE to focus initially on improving its marketing efforts to identify valuable customers and cross-sell opportunities.

In the early stages of a CoE, it is important to keep the focus somewhat narrow. The CoE can only bite off so much without getting a reputation for trying to do too much too soon—or fail to deliver tangible results and lose its credibility with the business units. The CoE needs an initial win and a success story to catch the attention of the business unit and encourage its participation and engagement with the CoE. As the CoE begins to establish its roles and relationships within the organization, its members will be better equipped to deal effectively with thorny internal politics. Limiting the scope of the CoE's influence, at first, allows the CoE to ensure continued buy-in and collaboration.

FINDING THE RIGHT FUNDING MECHANISM

Organizations often flounder when it comes to determining how to fund a CoE. You want business units to use the services, expertise, and advice of the CoE. Thus, charging for using the CoE is tricky. Business units within Department Level organizations, for instance, don't want to be charged to then be told they need to work at breaking down their information silos. It would be reasonable to be charged for consulting on the purchase of major analytics—the kind of consulting the business unit might have looked for outside the organization. But, in general, to acquire strong support for the CoE's toughest work—building an enterprise-wide view of data and changing culture to be data-driven—the CoE needs to be budgeted as a line item in the overhead budget. To make sure the budgeted dollars remain, the CoE's first task is to work with its executive sponsor to develop a set of metrics it will be measured on.

SELECTING THE RIGHT PERSONALITIES

There is no one right way to staff a CoE, or one specific mix of skills. Many staffing decisions are made as a result of completing an assessment of the current information management practices in the organization. The assessment will not only reveal the organizational maturity level but, more important, will also identify the organization's weaknesses and strengths that may impact its ability to achieve its business priorities. Identifying these weaknesses and strengths and conducting a capability gap analysis will enable the organization to figure out the proper ways to close gaps, address weaknesses, and leverage strengths. These are the essential first steps to identifying and designing the proper CoE organizational structure and identifying the required resources to staff it. In general, the key traits necessary for CoE resources are:

- Business, technical, and industry domain background
- Ability to translate business requirements into technical and IT processes
- Strong skills at working collaboratively with many groups
- Ability to listen to the business, technical, and personal requirements from the business users
- Excellent communication and personal skills
- Specialized skills determined by the focus and function

KEY TAKEAWAYS

- Secure executive-level sponsorship to lead and support the organization's effort not only initially, but throughout the information maturity journey.

- Evaluate the current organizational maturity to determine capabilities, weaknesses, and gaps that may prevent the organization from achieving its business objectives.

- Develop a strategy that outlines how the organization will address gaps and develop the required capabilities to achieve its business objectives.

- Evaluate the role of an enterprise Information and Analytics Center of Excellence that can lead and direct the organization's efforts, and develop the CoE organizational structure, engagement processes, and required skills.

- Develop a roadmap that will break down the required steps into reasonable and manageable phases that can be adopted by the organizational culture.

BEST PRACTICE ⚡ RAMPING UP YOUR CHANGE AGENT

Ultimately, CoEs should be part of a broader roadmap to address gaps and weaknesses in capabilities and in the current information management practices in an organization. The CoE can be your catalyst, your agent of change, and a key means of accelerating the organization's efforts to evolve into a higher maturity level.

As noted earlier, CoEs are not silver bullets, and they don't solve all problems. But when organizations think through the role and mission of a CoE and support it at the highest levels, the centers can produce significant value and tangible results.

Organizations should not establish a CoE just because it is a best practice approach to improve efficiency and alignment between business and IT. Don't do it because it seems like it is something you should do. A much better approach is to understand the concept and its strategic nature, something you learned about in reading this chapter. The next chapter focuses on how organizations can develop a business analytics strategy.

NOTE

1. Dan Ariely, *Predictably Irrational: The Hidden Forces That Shape Our Decisions* (New York: Harper Perennial, 2010).

7

Starting the Journey: Developing a Strategy and Roadmap to Guide Your Business Transformation

What we've learned so far: To improve an organization's maturity level, a business transformation effort is required to improve and align the capabilities of the organization's four pillars: people, information processes, technical infrastructure, and culture. Structuring and launching a business transformation initiative is a journey that should be well planned and executed. To plan the journey, organizations need to address three key requirements:

1. Secure continuous executive sponsorship.

2. Assess current capabilities and dynamics of the four organizational pillars (people, processes, technical infrastructure, and culture) using a structured maturity model to determine the starting/baseline and target points.

3. Align the capabilities of the four pillars with the organization's business objectives with the support of a Center of Excellence to develop the four pillars.

As you've read throughout this book, a business transformation strategy is necessary to make this happen.

KNOWING WHERE TO START

It is not easy to transform an organization, especially as it relates to information maturity. When an organization makes the decision to embrace information maturity, the "where to start" question isn't simple to answer. Should a Center of Excellence be chartered? Are there people on staff who can guide us? Will this require the help of an outside consultant? Everyone nods eagerly when you tell them how information, properly aligned, can help them make decisions quickly and effectively. But moving to more mature levels, breaking down silos, transforming the culture—this is tough stuff. It can't be done in a few months, or even a year or maybe several years. You need to start somewhere. And this is what this chapter is about: getting started.

Let's start by reviewing how two organizations successfully planned and executed their business transformation strategy, and the business results they managed to achieve.

RIYAD BANK'S ENTERPRISE BUSINESS INTELLIGENCE COMPETENCY CENTER

Riyad Bank is one of the largest financial institutions in the Middle East with US$49 billion in assets. It has 251 branches, including locations in Houston, London, and Singapore, along with 20 self-service branches and 2,600 ATMs. The bank has the best credit rating of any financial institution based in Saudi Arabia.

Challenges and Objectives

With the highest bank rating in Saudi Arabia, Riyad Bank was growing and experiencing many of the typical informational and organizational challenges such as information silos, business alignment, and the need for infrastructure enhancements and optimization. The bank was also launching a customer-centric initiative, and wanted to improve its information quality and its business performance monitoring capabilities.

Riyad Bank realized that a business transformation effort was needed to implement its customer-centric initiative. The bank needed to better understand its customers so it could develop and promote the appropriate financial products and services to the right customers, manage risk, and arm its decision makers with consistent and accurate information to help them make better decisions. The bank knew that a technology solution alone was not the answer.

Enterprise Plan with a Phased Approach

To effectively implement its customer-centric strategy, Riyad Bank used a comprehensive and enterprise-focused business transformation approach to evaluate the organization's maturity in developing and using information. The bank used the SAS information maturity model to evaluate its current capabilities, determine the target maturity level, and develop a roadmap to enhance its capabilities and reach the desired maturity level. The bank carefully evaluated the skills of its workforce, the current internal information processes, the capabilities and architecture of its information environment, and, of course, its internal culture. The investment in this evaluation enabled the bank to develop a roadmap to change its information management practices and operating model. The bank implemented organizational and business changes, including the establishment of an enterprise Business Intelligence Competency Center (BICC) to lead its business transformation effort. The focus of the BICC organization was not limited to business intelligence. It included all the analytical, performance management, and data integration efforts as well.

This BICC organization is one of the best practices implementations of the concept of the Enterprise Business Analytics Centers of Excellence that was explored in Chapter 6. Riyad Bank chose the name "BICC" for the implementation.

The bank also understood the expected business impact of all the new changes it was planning to introduce, and decided to take a phased approach to gradually roll out new capabilities and change the operating model and culture. To do that successfully, the bank used its business priorities and decided to focus on one critical business function first: its retail banking business unit.

Evolution and Expansion over Time

The BICC organization started with fewer than 10 resources, and quickly grew to a staff of 29 employees. The group included technical staff from the business units who had managed their unit's siloed information systems. The BICC organization reports to the Deputy CEO, who provides it with enterprise visibility and reach. "Our BICC team consists of a mix of business, analytical, and technical resources with a good business understanding of the operation and priorities of the business units we support," says Mr. Yassir Al-Suwais, Senior Vice President, Enterprise Business Intelligence Competency Center.

Initially the BICC organization focused on helping promote the use of the information to support business decisions, including a function devoted to change management and communication. "Now the role of the BICC organization started to shift towards delivering business advisory services by partnering with our business unit stakeholders and working together to figure out how we can apply ana-

lytics to expand our business and grow revenue," says Mr. Adil Belhouari, AVP and Manager of BICC Analytics & Data Mining group.

The keys to Riyad Bank's success with their BICC are:

- Comprehensive evaluation of current organizational capabilities provides a clear view of what needs to be done to change the current operating model and culture.

▓ A phased approach produces quicker business value and provides organizations with the flexibility to make adjustments to address changing business requirements and conditions.

Business Benefits from the New Organization

This wasn't just an exercise in using data. The bank had specific goals in mind. On the marketing side, it wanted to enhance cross-selling, attract new customers, increase sales, develop strategic partnerships for customer loyalty programs, and support channel activities. It wanted to do all this while decreasing the costs of marketing projects. During its short time in existence, the BICC organization has already increased cross-sell wins by 35 percent, helped the retail business unit to identify its most valuable customers, and launched programs to retain them. The team is now continuing to add value by using analytics to segment customers, develop retention, and churn models, and using LTV models to win back lost customers.

The bank's operations group specifically wanted to see if there was a less expensive way to keep ATMs adequately stocked with cash. The BICC team figured out how to reduce the amount of ATM dormant cash by 35 percent by optimizing its replenishment process. The BICC organization is also supporting the risk team in its effort to comply with Basel II and developing risk models to monitor and control risk.

These early successes represent comparatively simple wins—the low-hanging fruit of taking an enterprise-wide information approach.

To continue to succeed, Riyad Bank understood that it needed an enterprise-wide set of metrics. One of the BICC's current tasks is to survey business units and help develop a set of metrics that can measure the business value from the BICC contribution.

Future Expansion

The progress achieved by the BICC organization encouraged Riyad Bank's executives to continue its mission of evolving the organization's maturity level by investing in new enterprise-wide projects such as data quality management, big data analytics, and a customer experience analytics program.

E.SUN BANK'S CUSTOMER RISK VALUE ORGANIZATION

E.SUN is one of the leading banks in Taiwan, and was named by The Banker *as one of the top global 500 banking brands in 2013.*

E.SUN Bank developed a strategic Center of Excellence organization to improve its CRM marketing capabilities. The organization is called Customer Risk Value (CRV), and it was an expansion of an existing team that provided risk intelligence support. The most innovative approach in the E.SUN Bank case is how it is measuring the performance and business impact of this organization, as explained later in this section.

The CRV organization has 36 resources to support risk and marketing analytics requirements for the bank. The team is structured into three groups to handle Analytics CRM (ACRM), Operational CRM (OCRM), and an Analytical Data Warehouse. The groups within the CRV organization included three teams: Campaign Analytics, Data Mining, and Operational CRM.

E.SUN bank developed career paths to not only attract highly skilled resources, but also to develop and retain these critical resources by providing them with a well-defined path to develop their skills and grow their career potential. The career path covered both campaign and analytical data mining resources.

- The career path for campaign resources—data analytics → insighter → tactical planner → strategic planner → PM → consultant
- The career path for mining resources—data analytics → insighter → modeling → modeling resolution → modeling system or decision manager → consultant

E.SUN realized the importance of having the right talent. The bank developed a training program and was able to develop 95 percent of the skills and talents it needed. In addition, 20 percent of the CRV staff comes from the bank business units.

How the CRV Focus Evolved over Time

The CRV team was established in 2006 with an initial focus on the risk intelligence function. The team provided analytical services to support the risk team in making decisions. The focus of the CRV organization was expanded in 2008 to also support the marketing function. The CRV organization now supports the bank's effort to promote a customer-centric approach versus a product-centric approach. This approach required the development and extensive use of analytical methods and capabilities.

The team offered analytical services, including customer segmentations, propensity to buy analytical models, and other services to support the marketing team. The expansion continued to offer strategic services including campaign services, data mining, support for the OCRM function, and the development and maintenance of the Analytical Data Warehouse. The team is working closely with the business units and is using their business requirements to determine the proper content and structure of the Analytical Data Warehouse.

The CRV organization is now looking into the use of digital marketing analysis, online behavior analysis, and big data analytics.

How the CRV Organization Is Adding to E.SUN Bank

The CRV organization has been adding value to the organization since it was established. Some of the business benefits include:

- The analytical insight developed by the CRV team enabled the risk team to support the bank in growing its lending products to qualified customers by 60 percent. The CRV team was responsible for 25 percent of this growth.
- Reduced call center labor cost for campaign (e.g., from 130 to 25 call center employees).

E.SUN Bank groups the services offered by the CRV organization into three types. The bank uses these three project categories to measure the business ROI contributed by the CRV organization. The project categories are:

1. **Sales revenue-driven project type**: The CRV organization co-owns the P&L and sales quota with the business units. The

main business with significant growth includes personal loan, mail loan, and cross-sell insurance products. Sales revenues doubled using only 30 percent of the call center resources compared to previous performance figures.

2. **Consultative project type**: These types of projects focus on the strategic business value generated for E.SUN Bank, and not on generating immediate revenue (for instance, focusing on customer segmentation versus customer treatment strategy). Other technical projects include the development of analytical data marts and segment-specific analytical risk models. These projects are sometimes initiated by business units. The bank uses CRV members' utilization KPIs to ensure projects are completed on time and are producing high quality outcome within the assigned budget.

3. **Innovative project type**: The CRV organization runs two to three innovative projects per year. The innovative project is the most comprehensive project for the CRV organization. These projects cover conceptual phases and continue to produce actionable results. They are business-oriented projects and don't necessarily focus on technical areas.

SUCCESS STORY TAKEAWAYS

These two organizations applied some of the most aggressive and pragmatic approaches to achieve their business objectives. The internal visibility, clout, and performance management approach were essential to help these organizations become effective quickly. Their implementations are significantly improving the organizations' ability to develop and use business insight to support their objectives and decision-making process. The internal influence of these CoE organizations is deliberate, well planned, and supported by the executive team. The progress of these CoE organizations would not have been possible without the continuous support and monitoring from the executive team.

It is important, too, to point out that the success of these CoE organizations is also due to the banks' clarifying how these CoE organizations will work with the business units and the IT team. This is a key success factor.

And, finally, the CoE organizations are agents of change, gradually changing the decision-making culture. After the Riyad Bank CoE organization (BICC) was established and improved the basic reporting and analysis capabilities in many business units, it started to shift its focus toward delivering business advisory services to business stakeholders. The CoE analytical consultants started to work closely with business stakeholders to figure out how to apply analytics to expand the business and grow revenue based on accurate insight derived from information. This represents a key organizational maturity milestone in moving toward fact-based and analytically driven decisions and strategies. This is clearly a cultural change toward a higher maturity level.

APPLYING THE LESSONS FROM E.SUN AND RIYAD

No two organizations are alike. Their successes can't be lifted and grafted to your organization; they developed plans that were specific to their strengths and weaknesses. What applies to any organization is the approach used to arrive at this structure. And that brings us to the next topic: How can an organization develop a business transformation strategy to work for its unique requirements, environment, and culture? Let's explore the answer to this question in the following sections.

THE MOST IMPORTANT CHARACTERISTICS OF SUCCESSFUL BUSINESS TRANSFORMATION STRATEGIES

Before discussing the key components of a business transformation strategy, let's review what a good business transformation strategy should cover. There will be many unique requirements for each organization. However, all organizations should be mindful of the following requirements when developing a strategy. A strategy should:

- **Address more than just the technology**. The tendency of many organizations is to think of the technology first. There is no doubt that appropriate technology to apply analytics to generate business insight is needed. Technology alone will not resolve internal organizational and business challenges, nor will it achieve the long-term objectives of any business transformation strategy.

▪ **Create a repeatable process to generate business insight**. The strategy has to build a long-term foundation of well-planned and agreed-on repeatable processes. All business units will use these processes to interact and collaborate to generate and use business insight.

▪ **Evaluate current capabilities and interactions of the four organizational pillars**. Chapters 3, 4, and 5 covered the pillars: people, processes, technology, and culture. Understanding where your organization stands in regard to each pillar is crucial.

A STEP-BY-STEP LOOK AT THE KEY COMPONENTS

There are five key components of effective business transformation strategies:

1. Clear strategy objectives
2. Current and desired competencies and capabilities
3. Approach to achieve strategy objectives
4. Initial set of organizational initiatives to achieve objectives
5. Clear performance management KPIs agreed to by stakeholders

Clear Strategy Objectives

Internal and external triggers drive organizations to think about the need for a business transformation. They may include market pressure from the competition that makes organizations take a closer look at their internal capabilities and operating model. It could be the vision of a new executive who was brought in by the board to take the organization's operation to a higher level, new market, or new products. Or it may be that the internal information and organizational challenges have reached an intolerable level and are hindering the organization's progress. Whatever the trigger, the organization— and specifically the executive sponsor—has to think very carefully about what the organization needs to do and can do in a realistic and pragmatic way. The answer may be a set of objectives and priorities. It may be that the organization needs to improve its marketing functions and try to know its customers better, or it may be that the risk or fraud area is a critical function that needs to be managed better. It may be that the executive team recognized that the organization is not making sound decisions based on facts and needs to improve its capabilities to generate business insight.

These triggers start a conversation among stakeholders. The key is to recognize the difference between making localized improvements (limited to a particular business function) versus applying a comprehensive business transformation approach to outdated systemic and widespread practices. The objectives should be clearly defined and, more important, prioritized, since they will serve as the general guidelines and targets for any business transformation strategy.

Current and Desired Competencies and Capabilities

The objectives will tell us a lot about the final destination. Do we want to be the number one bank (by deposits) in China? Are we trying to be the Brazilian telco with the most innovative product mix? These goals will inform how you map your information maturity journey. And as in any journey you will need to know where you are right now. Organizations might think it is easy to understand what their current capabilities are. That assumption is probably inaccurate. Executives may know the organization's current capabilities, strengths, and weaknesses at a high level. For instance, the CEO knows that innovative ideas are generated regularly but take too long to reach the market. Trying to figure out why, though, is problematic. There might be a focus on the enterprise resource planning system not providing enough support when the real issue might lie in skill sets, cultural interactions, and organizational politics.

A comprehensive evaluation of the current capabilities and inter-actions of the four organizational pillars is not only essential, but will save the organization time, effort, and money down the road. Establishing a capability baseline that shows the strengths and weak-nesses of the people, processes, technical and information infrastruc-ture, and culture is an essential component of a well-planned business transformation strategy. The Information Evolution Model, explained in Chapters 3, 4, and 5, provides a structured approach to evaluate current capabilities and establish a capability baseline.

The strategy objectives provide a second key input to this process. Objectives should be used to determine the desired capabilities. For instance, if the organization wants to introduce and promote the use of analytics to support decisions and validate strategies, then it should work on developing new capabilities in analytical skills, accurate and consistent information, and analytical information data marts to sup-port analytics. Furthermore, the capabilities will also include devel-oping an analytical team or an Analytics Center of Excellence with a well-defined set of processes to allow the business units to tap into this talent to help them make better decisions. And, finally, changes to the organizational culture may be needed to ensure that the adoption and use of analytics is encouraged and supported. The Information Evolution Model can help you determine the desired target capabili-ties and maturity level based on the strategy objectives.

Approach to Achieving Strategy Objectives

By establishing your capabilities baseline, you understand where you are today. You have also outlined the desired capabilities you need to develop. What organizations need to do next is think about how to improve the capabilities baseline to develop the desired capabilities. Again, these capabilities must include all four organizational pillars.

Organizations should ask themselves the following key questions:

- What is the scope of the required effort to develop desired capabilities?
- Who will lead this effort?
- What type of organization should own the key development steps?

- Would an enterprise Center of Excellence be the appropriate organizational approach?
- What changes in the current operating model and processes are required?
- Where should we start?

Initial Set of Organizational Initiatives to Achieve Objectives

Business transformation effort takes time and should include a well-planned set of activities or initiatives sequenced in an implementation roadmap. Each initiative should improve the current capability baseline and move it closer to the desired capabilities. These capabilities must address the four organizational pillars. The collective business impact of all identified initiatives should move the organization toward achieving its strategy objectives.

For instance, if the organization is trying to introduce and promote the use of analytics across business units, some of the initiatives may include:

- **People and skills**: Determine what skills are needed, what skills the organization currently has, and the organization's potential to attract, hire, and retain the necessary talent.

- **Technical and information infrastructure**: Evaluate the effectiveness of the current information environment, data quality, historical data, and availability of analytical data marts.

- **Processes**: Review the current engagement model and interactions between business units to determine how critical analytical resources are utilized.

- **Culture**: Assess the awareness and knowledge of analytics and how it is currently being used.

The result of the process is to identify and prioritize initiatives needed to meet strategy objectives. This provides the building blocks of the implementation roadmap. From there, organizations can gain stakeholder buy-in for sequencing and supporting these initiatives. Now all you need to do is launch this process and follow the roadmap.

Clear Performance Management KPIs Agreed to by Stakeholders

The final component of an effective business transformation strategy is the development of performance management KPIs for each initiative. Many organizations tend to skip this critical step and find out later that many stakeholders have different opinions of the business transformation process and its success. With something that involves such an extensive amount of time, effort, and money, organizations have to define what success looks like.

The executive sponsor team should expect all the business and IT stakeholders to work together to develop, discuss, and agree to a set of performance management and success KPIs for each initiative. The key requirement here is to get *all* stakeholders to participate in this critical process. They must be part of it, and they all must agree to these KPIs. This will establish a collective sense of ownership and camaraderie among all stakeholders that is so important to the success of these long-term business transformation efforts.

IDENTIFYING A STARTING POINT

Organizations often struggle with identifying a starting point for both exploring current capabilities and engaging their business transformation efforts. All strategic initiatives that introduce a new way of doing business and change the current operating model in an organization should be viewed as an internal selling job to promote new business practices. To sell anything, organizations need to demonstrate proof of value to buyers. Introducing analytics, new technology, or new business practices as part of a business transformation effort is no exception. Consequently, identifying the starting point is critical to develop proof of value.

These are key questions that organizations should answer for each possible starting area or function:

- Does this area represent a high business priority for the organization that is sponsored by an executive?
- Do we have integrated and consistent data available for the selected area?

- Do we have sufficient integrated and consistent historical data—if the objectives include using analytics?
- Can we predict the potential outcome and would the outcome produce business value?
- Do we have the business domain, technical, and analytical skills we need to produce the expected outcome?

If the answers to these questions are yes, then the organization can start with the business function.

SUMMING IT ALL UP

Any kind of business transformation can seem a little overwhelming. Even with the Information Evolution Model, case studies, and compelling evidence of why you need to do this, wrapping your arms around the issue isn't easy. Here are guiding principles that can help you push past the institutional inertia to get your effort started.

- **Use a comprehensive organizational approach, no matter the pain.** When Riyad Bank decided to launch its customer-centric initiative, they knew that it would take more than just technology. Their comprehensive approach to evaluating their current organizational capabilities in skills, processes, technology, and culture provided them with a clear view of the nature, scale, and specific tasks needed to help the bank achieve its customer-centric model while enhancing the overall maturity level of the organization.
- **Use a phased approach that provides flexibility.** Another key lesson learned from the Riyad Bank experience is that it is beneficial to take a phased approach to quickly show value by focusing on one business function first, and then applying all the lessons learned from the first phase to other business functions.
- **Don't be tempted to employ the big bang approach.** If you are thinking, "Forget the piecemeal approach. We're going to analyze every nook and cranny of this organization," stop! It will take too long to show business value and the business requirements could change along the way. Adopting a phased

approach allows organizations to make quick adjustments to their plans to deal with changing business requirements.

▪ **Structure your organization's performance management and compensation to drive the desired behavior**. Performance management principles are needed to guide the operation of any business function, as well as to guide employees' performance. This is required for two reasons. First, it is a responsibility and obligation for a well-run organization to provide enough guidance to the workforce to help it complete its work successfully. Second, setting up appropriate employee and business function KPIs and how well employees are compensated are very effective ways to promote the desired behavior for the organization.

IN THE END, IT'S ABOUT BEING A LEADER

The world is a very different place than it was 10 years ago, and it will be a very different place a decade from now. Chances are the leading organizations in banking, communication, technology, retail, entertainment, and manufacturing in 2024 won't all have the same names as those today. Surviving and thriving will increasingly be dependent on the ability to see where the market is going much more quickly than the competition. The good idea won't be enough – it's what you do with that idea that will make or break your organization.

Agility and innovation are critical. But time-to-market is just as important to take advantage of market opportunities. This means knowing your customer. Organizations can now analyze their customers' behaviors, identify the most valuable customer segments, and determine their propensity to buy or churn with remarkable accuracy. They can then use this information to put in place proactive campaigns to retain valuable customers and cross-sell more products and services. That becomes critical to innovating, even disrupting, established markets.

Data-driven decision making underpins this customer knowledge. But being able to make decisions using information is dependent on taming organizational and information challenges and working on them simultaneously. It requires the enterprise to think differently and address systematic, political, technical, legacy, and other challenges comprehensively and with executive support. Visionary executives and leaders recognize the need for internal change to continue to compete in the market, and launch business transformation initiatives to introduce change and align the organizational pillars. The approach outlined in this book provides a framework for grappling with these issues.

Although the journey may seem difficult and lengthy, it can be tremendously rewarding—both to the organization and the people tasked with driving that change. Many organizations may choose to delay the journey by finding excuses or false hopes in tactical and limited solutions only to find out that the sooner they embrace the journey, the easier it is for them to get back on track and be competitive in the market. The practical guidance, ideas, and examples in this book should persuade your organization to pack its bags, chart its itinerary, and get going. There are risks and costs associated with any plan of action, but they are far less than the risks and costs associated with comfortable inaction.

Appendix: Snapshot of the Information Evolution Model

Chapters 3, 4, and 5 detail the levels of the Information Evolution Model. This appendix provides a brief overview of each level. It can help you begin to define what level your organization is at now—and what the next level looks like.

THE INDIVIDUAL LEVEL: GETTING ALONG ONE DAY AT A TIME

From the 30,000-foot perspective, the Individual Level organization is focused on getting the job done—now.

- **Business focus**. Sustain day-to-day operations and promote the business. The focus is completely driven by the need to react to tactical and immediate business requirements. Long-term strategies for the business unit or the enterprise are not a priority.

- **Data value**. Data is valued by some as a source of individual power and does provide limited value at the department level but questionable value for the enterprise. As long as data is perceived as correct for operational purposes—bills are accurate, orders are filled correctly—upper-level management is content.

- **Decision making**. Decisions are limited to day-to-day, operational decisions, such as shipping, invoicing, sales, and collections.

Most decisions are based on personal experience, intuition, or bravado with some reliance on information produced by Information Mavericks, typically on request.

- **Globalization**. The Individual Level organization's ability to operate at the global level and deal with different market conditions is very limited. This is due to the fact that the basic fundamental understanding of the organization's business and value chain is lacking at the enterprise level. Good understanding of the internal processes, the viability of the organization's products and services, and the organization's interactions and collaboration with its external partners are all essential requirements to enable the organization to operate on a global level. The inability to operate effectively at a global level may limit the organization's competitive advantage.

Infrastructure: Desktop Diversity

- **IT architecture**. There is no overall information architecture at the department level or the enterprise level. There may be pockets of strong operational systems such as manufacturing or production systems, but business performance information is produced by a collection of unconnected and unsophisticated desktop and personal productivity tools. As a result, there are many individual interpretations of business performance by the Mavericks. This is chaos in action.

  Individuals maintain their own data, tools, and methods. Tools used to generate reports and business metrics are rarely documented, and they may become orphaned when their creators leave the organization.

- **Intelligence tools**. Tool capabilities are limited to simple data extraction and reporting. Toolsets also include personal productivity tools, such as Excel and Microsoft Access. There are no technology standards at the department or enterprise level, and, therefore, sharing data is a challenge. If more sophisticated tools are used, it is only because ambitious, self-taught employees have acquired them.

- **Information access**. Information access is limited to those who know how to find the data and analyze it themselves or have access to an Information Maverick who can share the data. Distributing information for decision making is not a common practice. Consequently, decision makers do not always have access to reliable and consistent information and frequently rely on instinct. Multiple and inconsistent reports and business views create confusion and redundancy.

- **Analytics**. Very little advanced analytics technology is used. There may be infrequent use of analytics by individuals with the appropriate skills to meet ad hoc business requests.

- **Data management**. Data management depends on individual efforts of the Information Mavericks. Managing information is not viewed as a top business priority. As a result, there are many undocumented, unrepeatable, inconsistent data management efforts.

- **New technologies**. Organizations at this level are not able to take advantage of new advances in technology concepts and methodologies such as master data management, service-oriented architecture, or cloud computing. Implementing these technologies and methodologies requires an environment with a more mature level of collaboration.

Information Processes: Have It Your Way

- **Degree**. There is little emphasis on policies, practices, and standards around the collection, distribution, and use of information. Decision makers must rely on their own individual efforts to obtain information. In many cases, they must manually piece together information from many different individuals or sources. There is no defined or funded team with responsibility for supporting business users.

- **Consistency**. Consistent results, if they occur, are a fortunate accident. Two people in the same group, using the same information for much the same purpose, might do things differently. There are no departmental or organization standards.

Information Mavericks have developed their own processes to get information.

■ **Metrics**. Metrics are primarily focused on recent financial performance of the organization. The Individual Level organization does not generally collect and use other metrics such as customer satisfaction, internal efficiencies, and external market conditions. Most of the metrics are lagging metrics; that is, they focus on past performance.

■ **Governance**. General information management governance, if it exists, is limited to operational and financial systems. IT and data quality governance are rarely observed at an Individual Level organization. People who prize autonomy appreciate the lack of standard protocol.

■ **Outsourcing**. The culture at the Individual Level organization is heavily influenced by personal or individual objectives that greatly reduce the likelihood of outsourcing nonessential functions. Additionally, the lack of documented processes, standards, and policies introduces challenges in obtaining desired results.

■ **Change management**. There is resistance to change at many levels within the organization. Maintaining the status quo is an acceptable and desirable approach for an Individual Level organization. The emphasis on individualism tends to squelch any out-of-the box thinking.

People: Data Stars

■ **Skills**. The organization does not recognize the business value of hiring, motivating, and retaining individuals with critical thinking, technology, and analytical skills, except perhaps in the IT organization. Hiring practices and job categories do not typically reflect information management and analytical skills. Within business units, some people will bring information skills from their former jobs or pick them up on their own. These individuals may become Information Mavericks through their ability to analyze data and share it with decision makers.

▪ **Motivators**. Decision makers in these organizations are generally motivated by and focused on dealing with day-to-day crises within their own departments. They are not motivated to make decisions based on good quality information or consideration of other aspects of the organization.

▪ **Dynamics**. Information Mavericks may hold the enterprise hostage with their exclusive access to information. They will share their results (with their own personal interpretation), but not their process for obtaining them. Most other individuals have to base their decisions on instinct and experience.

Culture: Rugged Individualism

▪ **Rewards**. Rewards are subjective and often political, focused on individual excellence in day-to-day activities rather than contributions to corporate-level objectives. This reward structure creates internal competition for political favor and recognition, and does not reward information skills.

▪ **Adaptability**. The corporate mission and objectives are not well defined or communicated. Consequently, information management efforts are not aligned with corporate objectives.

Change is feared and shunned unless there is personal gain involved. Information Mavericks are especially resistant to change, because they stand to lose power or influence if they must forfeit their proprietary positions.

▪ **Collaboration**. In this politically charged organization, managers exercise a lot of command and control. Although they issue edicts, the Information Mavericks hold the day-to-day power, since they hold the key to the information that managers need.

There is little internal collaboration within or between business units. As a result, the organization's ability to respond to changes in market conditions is significantly reduced.

▪ **Innovation**. The environment is internally competitive. Thought leaders and innovators who propose anything outside the box are not encouraged or rewarded. They may, in fact, be viewed as a threat.

- **Internal collaboration**. Individual Level organizations are not in a position to leverage the diverse talents available in their environment because of the nature of their internal culture. These environments are very tactical and are not focused on how to maximize or improve their ability to use information and solve problems. Instead, they are occupied with the tactical nature of their day-to-day routine, and are content with very few individual efforts to manage information and provide answers to their operational concerns.

- **Analytical thinking**. Because information and critical-thinking skills are not readily available in all business units, decisions are often based on individual experience or gut instinct. Information management and analytical tasks are based on individual efforts that are scattered throughout the organization. These efforts are not coordinated or shared between business units, and are typically focused on tactical day-to-day operations. There is little emphasis on using analytics or nonfinancial metrics to drive decisions and set strategies.

- **Social responsibility**. The social pressure at an Individual Level organization is not viewed as a top priority. There is no significant organizational commitment or funding dedicated to social responsibility initiatives beyond the possibility of pet projects.

DEPARTMENTAL LEVEL: THE CONSOLIDATED ORGANIZATION

Silos of information are the hallmark of this IEM level. They are well guarded and enthusiastically supported.

- **Business focus**. Each individual department or business unit drives toward its own consistency and success. The focus is on meeting the short-term or tactical requirements of the business unit with little or no consideration of enterprise strategy or the performance of other business units.

- **Data value.** Information is valued for achieving department-level goals but rarely has an impact on a corporate decision, nor is it valued as a corporate asset. Users realize data quality is important, but they control quality only in their own domains—often by applying unique rules, manually correcting known errors, and filling in the gaps with their own knowledge. There is no big picture.

- **Decision making.** Decisions revolve around myopic departmental goals and requirements. Most decisions are made in departmental islands. Enterprise decisions are pushed up to higher levels where executives can add their insights.

  At the enterprise level, good decision making is hindered by the lack of consistent reporting from the departments. The available information provides differing views of performance because there are no standards or adherence to standards for data, reporting, analysis, or tools.

- **Globalization.** A Departmental Level organization may have limited ability to operate at a global level. The organization's ability may be limited to those business units and departments that have some control and understanding of their information management processes. Consequently, many global opportunities to leverage the organization's products and services may be missed, or explored and managed with great difficulties.

Infrastructure: Departmental Tools and Standards

- **IT architecture.** Hardware and networking standards have been established across the enterprise, but each department uses its own tools and data standards. Except for basic infrastructure, there are no enterprise-wide technology standards or frameworks. In fact, it is very fragmented. There might be dozens of departmental databases on servers stored in offices and maintained by individuals, most of them unknown to IT and some even unsupported by their vendors.

- **Intelligence tools.** Each department acquires and uses its own business intelligence tools—niche or proprietary solutions acquired to address a specific function, such as campaign management, supplier evaluation, or budgeting. These tools might be quite sophisticated but they cannot be used for broader applications outside the department without discussions and negotiations between business units. Without the oversight or control of an enterprise architecture group, redundancy of tools and applications remains a problem.

▪ **Information access.** Departmental data marts assemble data from the group's users and make it available in numerous reports, but these reports often present conflicting results across departments and provide limited context. How do the figures relate to real business issues?

Worse, needed information might be owned by other departments, and there is no formal way of accessing it. There is some collaboration via meetings, memos, and simple file sharing, but understanding the data still requires the tribal knowledge and goodwill of information gatekeepers. There is too much time spent finding and assembling information; too little time is spent making sense of it.

▪ **Analytics.** Analytics expertise is limited to individuals or small groups contained within a department or business unit. Niche tools with specialized analytic capabilities are used, for example, in marketing or campaign optimization or cash flow forecasting, but their use cannot usually expand beyond that specialized function.

▪ **Data management.** Standards may be provided but not mandated or adhered to, so there are a lot of different departmental deployments of data management techniques. There is a lack of consistent enterprise data stewardship effort, which is why there is no consistency beyond the department level. For example, customers, suppliers, and partners are defined differently or given different account codes across departments. Although the data are available, it is very hard to get a reliable, consistent view of how the organization as a whole interacts with the customer.

▪ **New technologies.** Departments do adopt and use new technologies, but their adoption is inconsistent and limited to their department. Some departments may have the appropriate skill sets and appetite for early adoption of systems to suit their needs, while other departments are more conservative in their approach. The result is unmanaged, inconsistent, and inefficient utility of the technology.

Information Processes: Well Defined at the Departmental Level

- **Degree**. Information is collected, assembled, accessed, and tracked on a departmental level. Data acquisition processes are separate from analysis and reporting, and many users receive reports on a systematic basis. De facto groups may evolve to become providers of reports and analyses for the department or business unit. This responsibility emerges because there is no corporate Center of Excellence. Their perspective is limited to requirements and practices of the department.

    Data management processes are fairly well defined within each department but not across departments. Since analysis is based on a myopic view, it will not accurately reflect influences from outside the department. There is also much duplication of effort, and departmental information must be manually consolidated to get an enterprise view.

- **Consistency**. Although there might be uniform hardware, networks, and software in place, this infrastructure is not used consistently. Even the simplest things, such as the definition of a "customer" or "sale," can vary by business unit. It is hard to generate an enterprise view that crosses organizational boundaries.

- **Metrics**. There is a heavy focus on static reporting of operational measures, such as gross margins, total revenue, total expense, or inventory on hand. Business analysts perform some interactive analysis to distill other performance measures, but only at a departmental level.

- **Governance**. If enforced, enterprise rules are left to interpretation by individual departments. Departmental organizations are characterized by a strong departmental autonomy and lack of emphasis on enterprise governance and policies.

▪ **Outsourcing**. The availability of documented departmental standards and processes makes it possible for individual departments to outsource functions, much like the adoption of technology. Each department may use preferred providers, but there is little corporate governance of this activity, limiting the advantages for economies of scale and consistent quality and vendor management.

▪ **Change management**. Change occurs at an inconsistent pace and depends on each department's appetite for change.

People: Subject Matter Experts and Gatekeepers

▪ **Skills**. The job of subject matter expert (or business analyst) has been established within departments, and Information Mavericks have naturally migrated to those jobs. Subject matter experts spend the majority of their time preparing and integrating information and preparing reports that put the best spin on the data.

They are valued and paid for their information skills, even though they are not explicitly IT workers. Training, when it is provided, is done to satisfy departmental needs rather than any enterprise program for information skills training at the business unit level.

▪ **Motivators**. Team players thrive in this type of organization. They have strong managers who defend the department and create internal cohesion. Those with an interest in information management are recognized and appreciated for their skills.

▪ **Dynamics**. Team members work well together, but they are challenged when asked to work cooperatively with other departments. After all, those are competitors in the internal corporate struggle for power, recognition, and budget.

Culture: "Us versus Them"

- **Rewards**. Within departments, managers and subject matter experts have vested interests in controlling departmental data. Subject matter experts have emerged as the rightful owners of "good" data for their department and are rewarded for their ability to advance departmental agendas. They know how to use that data as "proof" of departmental needs and accomplishments. Incentives are based on meeting departmental goals, which may or may not be in line with the best interests of the enterprise. People are told they are empowered, but how empowered can they be if they do not have direct access to information?

- **Adaptability**. Change is embraced when it results in political or self-improvement gain for the department—or if it takes place in someone else's department (especially if it creates an opportunity to grab some of their resources). Change is viewed as a threat if it disrupts the department's own carefully groomed processes or if it requires disparate functional units to work together. Departments might actively resist change that benefits other groups or distracts them from their own missions, even if the organization as a whole would benefit. Even under the best of circumstances, change is poorly communicated, cautiously approached, and limited in results.

- **Collaboration**. Staff and funding are dedicated to departmental objectives, with the hope that the entire enterprise will be better off. However, the department focus creates an us-versus-them mentality. Every business unit protects data as its unique intellectual property. No one really wants to share. After all, to give away your knowledge is to give away some of your value and political position. In this top-down management structure with a strong team-first perspective, decisions can be very politically oriented.

- **Innovation**. Thanks to internal competition among departments, the culture is politically charged and somewhat distrusting.

Department heads are focused on making their departments shine rather than on making the organization shine. Therefore, people who think outside the box might be tolerated. However, their good ideas might not get very far, because exploring new ideas outside the assigned department is seen as nonproductive.

- **Internal collaboration**. Since Departmental Level organizations are characterized as siloed environments, they can only leverage the diverse talent and skills of their workforce in each specific silo or organizational unit. Individual business units and groups will benefit when they manage to bring together different skills to focus on solving the business challenges faced by each group. However, they will miss the opportunity to benefit from the cross-functional collaboration between business units, which will benefit the entire organization.

- **Analytical thinking**. A more organized use of analytical thinking and analytical technology will start to emerge in some business units as they try to understand their silo business view. The development of business unit information standards and policies provides an opportunity to apply analytical thinking and use analytical technology to manage and optimize the operation of each business function. However, these organizations will miss out on the value of applying analytics to analyze business performance across functions and groups to understand more comprehensively the performance of the entire enterprise.

- **Social responsibility**. The commitment to social responsibility is limited to individual efforts by some business units. A tangible enterprise strategy and impact on social responsibility and sustainability may be limited due to the lack of internal collaboration between business units and functions.

THE ENTERPRISE ORGANIZATION: A COMMON SENSE OF PURPOSE

When organizations reach the Enterprise Level they are much better equipped to take advantage of data and use it to drive business decisions.

- **Business focus.** Enterprise business performance is the main focus and driver. There is now a set of common corporate strategies and tactics, and each group understands its role in executing those tactics and the correlation among business units. Performance is now managed based on an informed, comprehensive view of all operations across the enterprise.

- **Data value.** Information is seen as a critical strategic asset, just as important as tangible, operational assets. Everyone understands that integrated information is essential to run the business. The organization has managed to integrate internal and external information successfully across business units and functions to create an enterprise view of the operation.

  For the first time, the organization understands its business value chain. Managers and staff also appreciate the importance of data quality.

- **Decision making.** Integrated enterprise information is now available to all decision makers across the enterprise. Decisions such as engaging new suppliers or launching campaigns to support dormant markets are focused around managing the value chain.

  All decision makers have access to accurate enterprise data and are empowered to make decisions using the information assets available to them. Decision makers can identify alternatives and act on information from a truly enterprise-wide perspective, and their decisions now reflect enterprise goals and objectives.

- **Globalization.** The Enterprise Level marks a significant milestone that increases the organization's ability to operate at the global level. Enterprise Level organizations are in a much better position to engage in the global market because they have developed a clearer understanding of their business model and value chain.

Infrastructure: Integrated across the Enterprise

- **IT architecture.** Moving beyond stand-alone and black box tools in the departments, this organization has achieved an integrated enterprise information platform. An enterprise repository of integrated data stores and manages all information from disparate databases, proprietary tools, and external sources. Enterprise-standard tool sets and applications manage data extract/transform/load (ETL) processes, data quality routines, analysis, and information delivery. Processes are defined for evaluating and implementing new architecture designs and practices, like service orientation, web services, and virtualization.

A central group has established at least a high-level enterprise data model that defines common measures, definitions, data standards, and metadata (data about data) for the whole organization. In this well-managed environment, central governance is maintained, all actions are tracked for compliance purposes, and all information assets are protected.

- **Intelligence tools.** This organization has made a concerted effort to manage and rationalize disparate data and tools across departments and business units. To maintain its enterprise view, the organization uses a standardized set of technologies, including data integration and management, reporting, distribution, analytics, and performance management. As a result of this effort, corporate memory, once reliant on operational processes, has now transitioned into a robust information system.

- **Information access.** Now that information resides in central data repositories, it is available to decision makers at all levels of organization, not just the original data "owners" or the executives. Furthermore, it has been cleansed through standard data-quality routines, so users can have confidence in the results. Decision makers now have access to information that represents "one version of the truth," presented to them with contextual relevance.

Users have access to the data through interfaces tailored for their specific needs and skill sets. Executive dashboards, summary information with drill-down capability for business managers, ad hoc query for business analysts, and sophisticated model development for quantitative analysts are examples of the flexibility provided. As a result, more users than ever exploit information with confidence and make more accurate decisions.

■ **Analytics**. The use of analytics has now extended beyond the department and business unit specialization and moved to the enterprise level. Analysts from various business units now have access to integrated enterprise data and can analyze it to understand various aspects of the business and enrich the value of information used by decision makers.

Now that the organization has integrated enterprise data available in analytical data marts, analysts can focus more on the analysis and less on finding and preparing data. With data available from across the enterprise and external sources, the results of analyses can be framed in broader context.

Analysis and visualization methods distill meaningful insights from enterprise data, without requiring business users to become statisticians.

■ **Data management**. Enterprise data management is driven by business requirements. The organization is considering operational business intelligence to address data latency in the context of those business requirements.

Enterprise Level organizations have established enterprise data governance, identified data stewards, and laid the foundation for a master data management program. Processes are in place to enforce data standards. The organization is better able to comply with external reporting requirements, such as Sarbanes-Oxley, Basel II, IFRS, GAAP, SEC, Solvency II, FDA, and other regulations and regulatory bodies.

■ **New technologies**. The adoption of new technologies is a managed process at the enterprise level. The organization is systematic in how technology is acquired, deployed, and maintained while still allowing departments to retain necessary autonomy to meet their individual business needs. This governed approach enables the organization to explore newer technology options, such as in-database processing, in-memory processing, Software as a Service, cloud computing, Advanced analytics, Big Data analytics, mobile computing, or Open Source.

Information Processes: Well-Defined across the Enterprise

- **Degree**. Information management concepts are applied and accepted. Data management processes are well defined, resulting in a shared view of operations and a reliable foundation for analysis. Processes to obtain information for decision making are well defined and detailed—technologies, people, plans, tasks, and responsibilities.

  Staff members can see exactly how they contribute to the business. Now that the organization has a holistic view of the enterprise, it starts to see duplicate, overlapping, and inefficient processes.

- **Consistency**. Enterprise governance is enforced, and data consistency is paramount. Centers of Excellence are in place to ensure consistent data definitions, data collection, data quality, analytics, and information delivery to support business objectives.

  Departmental and business unit information processes now align with enterprise objectives and with each other.

- **Metrics**. The organization now defines and tracks metrics related to overall business performance and the value chain. Departmental and enterprise metrics are more widely available to decision makers. Key performance indicators (KPIs) go beyond financial metrics to include measures such as comparative growth, customer satisfaction, internal process efficiency, and employee development.

- **Governance**. The organization has institutionalized governance to cover areas such as data quality, internal and external reporting, information life cycle management, data retention and disposition, information security and privacy policies, applications and tools, and intellectual property. These organizations have a much stronger handle on information governance.

- **Outsourcing**. Standards and processes are in place to use business priorities and core competencies to determine which business functions can be outsourced. Other standards determine how vendors are selected, terms are negotiated, and quality of deliverables is managed. Controls are in place for the bidirectional movement of data and information to and from vendors.

- **Change management**. Enterprise objectives are the drivers for change throughout the organization and within departments. Objective-driven changes are more readily adopted throughout the organization.

People: Knowledge Workers Encouraged to Work with Data

- **Skills**. The organization uses an up-to-date set of defined job categories to guide staffing initiatives. The organization actively seeks to recruit people with the targeted technical and information skills. The workforce contains a high percentage of knowledge workers—team players who have domain knowledge and understand corporate goals. Career development programs are widely used to keep employees current with new skills, technologies, and techniques.

- **Motivators**. Employees are encouraged to make fact-based decisions, based on the availability of complete and accurate information in the Enterprise Level organization. Exceptional information skills are rewarded accordingly because the organization places a high value on information.

- **Dynamics**. Employees at this level are aligned with enterprise goals. This alignment reduces the interdepartmental competitiveness typical in these organizations; every employee is driving toward the same destination.

Culture: All for One

- **Rewards**. The reward structure encourages users to comply with enterprise information standards. At this level, it is no longer acceptable to run wild and free with independent tool sets and methods. The organization especially prizes employees with exceptional skills in information management. The organization has defined career paths for information experts and provides ongoing training and organizational development to foster excellence.

- **Adaptability**. There is a strong drive by employees to obtain a clear and accurate view of operations, which requires a greater level of adaptability compared to the Departmental Level. Employees are now willing to share information and knowledge among themselves and across business units as long as the causes and benefits to the organization are well communicated.

- **Collaboration**. Multidisciplinary teams come together to solve corporate issues, and then are reshaped when the work is done. Employees may be temporarily assigned to cross-departmental teams in a way that best utilizes their skills and job functions. As a result, the workforce becomes adaptable; team members can work with anyone to get the job done.

- **Innovation**. Everyone is focused on the health of the enterprise and on producing high-quality data and analytics for strategic value. Employees are starting to think strategically, and a lot of ideas are being generated; more reliable information is made available. Some ideas make it to fruition, but with no real consistency because there is no formal means for evaluating or prioritizing them.

- **Internal collaboration**. Reaching the Enterprise Level marks the first opportunity for the organization to take advantage of its diverse collection of talent and expertise. The environment provides the opportunity for organizations to maximize the value of the collective and diverse expertise of its workforce and channel it to focus on understanding its value chain at the enterprise level. Enterprise Level organizations are willing to integrate a collection of multitalented individuals with multicultural skills covering critical thinking, technology, and analytics to focus on solving enterprise business objectives.

- **Analytical thinking**. Enterprise Level organizations focus on managing organizational performance based on an informed, comprehensive understanding of the enterprise value chain. The organization as a whole places more emphasis on critical thinking and analytical skills, which are made more available for cross-departmental initiatives. The availability of reliable enterprise information is feeding data-driven decision making.

- **Social responsibility**. The availability of comprehensive and accurate enterprise information drives organizational self-awareness. For the first time, the organization begins to establish strategies to address its social responsibility and sustainability goals.

THE OPTIMIZE LEVEL ORGANIZATION: ALIGNED AND READY

The Optimize Level organization is a well-oiled machine that has a clear picture of its value to customers and can adapt to any market change or condition with sufficient and continuous commitment. The organization has built on the integrated information environment it created at the Enterprise Level to further (and continually) optimize market alignment, business decisions, and processes.

The progression from the Enterprise Level to the Optimize Level is a fluid one, because it requires no significant overhaul on any dimension, just incremental enhancements in each. However, this level represents the point at which organizational focus can shift from collecting and integrating data to gaining genuine value and business insight from that data.

- **Business focus**. Organizations will start building on the integrated infrastructure developed at the Enterprise Level and the clear visibility of their value chain. They begin to optimize every aspect of their business function by driving the cost out and maximizing profit. The organization becomes more in touch with external market conditions and can foresee the slightest shift in expectations and realign the organization accordingly—while always improving the efficiency and effectiveness of related processes.
- **Data value**. Information is tightly woven into the fabric of the business and is highly valued as a strategic asset. Integrated

enterprise information is essential to identifying potential areas of efficiency gain.

There is an appetite for more data than ever because the organization monitors and analyzes structured and unstructured data from many sources: markets, customers, partners, suppliers, and even newer social networking sources like blogs and wikis.

▪ **Decision making.** Decision makers use integrated enterprise data to optimize their value chain. For example, decisions focus on optimizing how the organization is dealing with its suppliers, customers, and partners.

Decision makers at various levels focus on optimizing the business function they are responsible for with a clear understanding of the impact of their decisions on other business units. The decision-making environment is so agile that it can react quickly to the nonstop changes that happen in today's economy.

▪ **Globalization.** Optimizing the organization value chain represents the main focus of a Level 4 organization. The optimization process spans all aspects of the organization including its operations in various markets. Level 4 organizations are not only able to operate very efficiently in the global market, but also able to improve their bottom line in every market.

Infrastructure: Anywhere, Anytime Intelligence

▪ **IT architecture.** A Level 4 organization will evaluate and optimize its IT infrastructure to eliminate duplicate functions and processes. There are concerted efforts to identify and separate IT infrastructure functions that should be centralized from those that should be left to the business units. The objective is to increase the autonomy and flexibility for decision makers in business units while maintaining control over areas that should be governed by enterprise-wide rules and standards, such as security, data quality, and governance.

The organization also expands its IT infrastructure to increase collaboration with partners and customers, allowing them access to certain organizational data. The infrastructure is more open to integrate external data and contact channels to optimize insights for decision makers.

The infrastructure is reliable and fault tolerant, and data quality processes are widespread. The metadata model documents the entire business process, value, and strategy. Everything is transparent. A "closed-loop" infrastructure feeds results back into the system to create a continuous learning environment.

- **Intelligence tools**. The use of business intelligence tools goes way beyond drill, sort, filter, and rank—the calculations and tallies that are often mistakenly called analytics. Extending the value of the Enterprise Level analytical tools, users can predict future outcomes of interest; explore and understand complex relationships in data; and model customer behaviors and processes.

  Business intelligence tools model work-flow interactions to develop new and improved business processes. They monitor cause-and-effect relationships to continue finding opportunities to improve. They examine customer information to detect patterns that predict future behavior. And they get answers in real time, or close to it.

  In fact, information has become so automated and integral to the business that it is just something employees expect to be there when they need it, just like their desks and chairs.

- **Information access**. Organizations have an increased focus on information personalization. They make concerted efforts to determine the type and format of information needed by each information consumer category. Furthermore, special attention is given to the method and technology used to deliver that information. The objective is to match the information needs and skill level of users with the delivery method and content. Streamlining this process is essential to accelerate the optimization effort that characterizes a Level 4 organization.

  Critical external partners now have access to organizational data that enables them to work more collaboratively with the organization. Organizations provide their customers with more information to optimize and personalize the relationship.

- **Analytics.** The IT infrastructure is able to provide advance analytical capabilities such as optimization, forecasting, and predictive capabilities. The Level 4 organization is now focused on combining domain and analytical skills with these technical capabilities to optimize business performance and drive out cost and inefficiencies in the process.

- **Data management.** Additional enterprise data management effort is driven by optimization requirements that center on how the organization works with partners, customers, and suppliers. A strong focus on optimizing the organization value chain leads business users and decision makers to produce new data management practices constantly. Dynamic data management processes are in place to address the changing requirements. Centers of Excellence may play a significant role in enabling a Level 4 organization to be agile enough to meet new data management requirements.

- **New technologies.** The optimized nature of the Level 4 organizations accelerates their adoption of new technologies and concepts, especially those technologies that strengthen the relationships with customers, partners, and suppliers. Furthermore, Level 4 organizations are more aware and concerned about social networking media and may be more willing to incorporate insights from these media into their corporate database. Text analytics and social media analytics are used to extract insights from these media as part of the optimization process. The governed approach established in the Enterprise Level to evaluate the adoption of emerging technologies becomes more critical to continue to support optimization objectives.

Knowledge Process: Continuous Improvement

- **Degree.** Information processes established at the Enterprise Level are now expanded to provide a closed-loop feedback to enable optimization of internal and external functions. Best practices are captured to prevent repeated mistakes. This is the true "learning organization." Project experience is captured and cataloged, and new project teams start by checking out these corporate experiences.

Level 4 organizations put in place new information processes that govern how external information sources are integrated with organizational data. External information sources include suppliers, partners, social media, distribution channels, and, more importantly, customers.

- **Consistency**. Level 4 organizations make wider use of Centers of Excellence, which now focus primarily on optimization and enterprise information management in addition to data integration and quality.

  Consistent processes, tools, and information enable business units and decision makers to better analyze the relationships and dependencies between various business functions, which is essential for optimizing the value chain. For example, if combining two items on a promotional web page doubled sales of the cross-sell item, that knowledge can be quickly applied to in-store displays.

- **Metrics**. Because value chain optimization is the driving goal, a Level 4 organization's metrics reflect a more outward focus than ever before. The organization defines and tracks measures across time periods for the entire business value chain, such as employee productivity, sales growth rate, customer satisfaction, time to market, and adoption rate of new products and customers.

  Furthermore, there is an increased emphasis on analyzing the cause-and-effect relationships among performance metrics. To optimize, the Level 4 organization must dedicate an increased level of effort toward understanding root causes and key drivers of its performance.

- **Governance**. The strong governance framework established at the Enterprise Level has expanded to include relationships, information exchange, and processes with partners, customers, and suppliers.

■ **Outsourcing**. Better understanding of the value chain and the strong emphasis on optimizing their business performance enables the Level 4 organization to define its core competencies and identify functions that can be outsourced. This effort enables the organization to focus on outsourcing functions that are not core to its business.

■ **Change management**. Now that change is a core competency of the organization, new processes are put in place around optimizing the enterprise performance. The organization models work-flow interactions and analyzes results in the context for continuous process improvement.

People: Self-Managing Knowledge Workers

■ **Skills**. A Level 4 organization enriches its job family with new categories that focus on analytics, forward thinking, and performance management with wide-spanning authority and accountability. Critical thinking skills are vitally important, to monitor market data and analyze what it means to the organization's entire value chain.

　　Not surprisingly, the Optimize Level organizations face challenges in recruiting and retaining the right resources and skills. They often make significant investments in training and retaining their workforce. In many roles, information management and analytical thinking skills are required for advancement.

■ **Motivators**. A Level 4 organization permits more autonomy and empowerment among its skilled employees. Clear rewards are offered for employees who can think out of the box to achieve greater optimization. For an achievement-oriented individual, these organizations can be very gratifying places to work.

■ **Dynamics**. Level 4 knowledge workers are very focused on incremental process improvement. There is a strong commitment to process improvement and optimization. Peer groups are formalized across departments; these groups get together for brainstorming sessions that can lead the entire organization into new market dynamics. Employees and decision makers leverage information and use analysis, trending, pattern analysis, and predictive results to increase effectiveness and market share.

Culture: Thriving on Change

- **Rewards**. The compensation system is structured primarily around improving business performance. The organization expects employees to apply critical thinking, perform validation of assumptions, and determine root causes as bases for decisions. A well-communicated reward system is in place to reward employees who operate in this manner.

- **Adaptability**. Change is a core competency and is viewed as an opportunity, not a threat. The information architecture is adaptive, and so are job descriptions, accountabilities, organizational structure, work flow, and processes. That is a good thing, because change is rapid, iterative, and continuous—just as it is in the markets the organization serves.

- **Collaboration**. The environment promotes widespread sharing of internal and external information across business units and functions, providing a broad context for communities of interest to share their experiences and fine-tune the business. This culture of community now extends outside the organization to include customers, suppliers, and partners.

- **Innovation**. With a participative management style, the culture is very collaborative and supportive. Strategic thinkers are prized as visionaries, and their ideas are given a chance to fly. Some of these ideas will flop, but mistakes are not punished; they are viewed as learning experiences. The culture embraces the permission to fail when exploring new hypotheses and assumptions. The organization is so agile that missteps can be easily foreseen or overcome—and prevented from recurring.

  This supportive attitude works both ways. People are willing to accept the concept of compromise for the good of the organization if they know the organization is willing to compromise for them.

- ▣ **Internal collaboration.** To tackle difficult business problems, Level 4 organizations form diverse teams, combining expertise from various business functions in ways they've never done before. Critical analytical, business, and technical skills are leveraged to focus on optimizing the enterprise value chain. Level 4 organizations managed to identify, document, and distribute information about their enterprise value chain in the previous level. The process of mobilizing diverse talent may be facilitated by enterprise information management Centers of Excellence. These centers make that talent available to all business units.

- ▣ **Analytical thinking.** There is a higher focus on the value and use of analytics to optimize the current enterprise value chain established in the previous level. Decisions are always based on analytics that not only explain what was but reliably predict what will be, using quantitative and qualitative inputs. "Should we invest in this new product?" "Will this process improvement be worth it?" Answers to such questions emerge from sophisticated decision support tools, such as predictive modeling using activity-based costing to calculate the return on investment (ROI) of process changes and risk management to determine whether to chase a new opportunity.

- ▣ **Social responsibility.** Level 4 organizations are in a much better position to implement effectively their strategies to address their social responsibility and sustainability goals. Executing their strategies is facilitated as a component of their commitment and focus to optimize their enterprise performance and value chain.

THE INNOVATE LEVEL: SPAWNING AND SUPPORTING NEW IDEAS

The Innovate Level organization extends the value of previous evolutionary stages. This organization spawns new ideas as a matter of course and institutionalizes innovation in a manner similar to a think tank. This organization understands what it does well and applies this expertise to new areas of opportunity. There seem to be no limits to the new ideas that employees put forth, ideas that bring revenues from new sources. Some of the most inventive ideas are gleaned from other industries and unlikely inspirations.

- **Business focus**. There is a deliberate effort to sustain growth by constant innovation by maximizing the organization's competencies, intellectual property, and resources. Top-line revenues grow by applying core competencies to new products, markets, and business models—which propels the organization to market leadership. They have the agility to respond to change in markets.

- **Data value**. The Innovate Level organization demands more value from the data than what is offered by its own internal data. The data value is an essential tool for uncovering and exploring new opportunities and driving innovation. The organization explores data not only from its own operations and markets, but from other spheres where innovation might be found. The organization has confidence in its data and is able to use it to accurately model likely outcomes and effectively manage risk as it explores new products and markets.

- **Decision making**. An increased focus on innovation characterizes the types of decisions made by these organizations. Decision makers at various levels put an increasing effort on differentiating their products and services from their competitors, and on expanding into new markets and product lines.

  Everyone in the organization is encouraged to offer up new ideas constantly, which are routinely modeled in a simulated environment to identify the ones that will drive the organization forward. Groups with various competencies are formed to analyze and prototype new products and services. Go/no-go decisions are based on sophisticated descriptive and predictive analytics that include data from the entire value chain—from sources inside and outside the organization.

- **Globalization.** A principal focus of organizations at this level is innovation that is driven by a well-defined and aggressive internal process that encourages prototyping, piloting, and exploration in new markets. These organizations dominate their industries in market share, and are very successful competitors in the global market.

Infrastructure: A Support Network for Innovation

- **IT architecture.** The integrated, enterprise-wide IT architecture serves as a support network for creativity. It includes systems to assemble any type of internal and external information that could spawn new ideas, manage the pipeline of new ideas, and implement ideas that are deemed worthy to pursue. The infrastructure accepts structured and unstructured data in a variety of media and languages, such as databases, text documents, graphics, e-mail, and digitized voice communications.

  Proposals and pilot projects are documented, categorized, and easily accessible for reference and use. Post pilot reviews are documented and made available to all who might learn from them.

- **Intelligence tools.** Predictive analytics are used extensively to model the future—to identify potential ideas quickly, rule them out or approve them, and minimize the risk of moving forward with any of them. "What if" becomes a daily question, and analytics provide reliable answers based on quality information. Risk management systems and human capital management systems take on new life. The organization also adds an integrated application to manage the pipeline of new projects.

- **Information access.** User access at the Innovate Level depends on role. Many employees will focus on maintaining Enterprise and Optimize Level efficiencies. A smaller number will focus on creating change—identifying and seizing on new opportunities. These people will have widespread access to many data sources from a broad selection of industries, areas of interest, and backgrounds.

- **Analytics**. Innovate Level organizations focus on exploring new ideas, products, and services, and use many different types of analytical technologies and methods. These capabilities are used to conduct different types of analysis such as cost benefit analysis, customer behaviors and propensity to buy products and services, external market data, and so forth.

- **Data management**. The data management environment and effort are very dynamic and set up to expect and facilitate the need to analyze and explore new business and market opportunities. Data management efforts enable analysts to regroup and restructure products and services data in different ways to analyze future opportunities.

- **New technologies**. Innovate Level organizations have a strong commitment to explore new market opportunities. This commitment provides them with more flexibility in exploring new cutting edge technologies, pushing the envelope of existing capabilities, and pioneering their own new methodologies and concepts.

Knowledge Process: Managing Constant Renewal

- **Degree**. In addition to the well-defined processes that provide cross-functional collaboration at the Enterprise Level and optimization at the next level, the Innovate Level organization adds new processes and policies for managing innovation.

  All information types, measures, and experiences are applied to develop insights that lead to innovation. A project incubation process ensures the growth of many new ideas and moves them quickly into prototype and pilot stages. The results of innovation are routinely managed, evaluated, and communicated. The innovation pipeline is analyzed just like a portfolio of risk. The organization always understands such issues as technology readiness, potential barriers, and the impact of a new project on existing processes.

- **Consistency**. Alignment with enterprise goals is a given by now. Beyond mere consistency, Innovate Level organization processes are self-learning and self-tuning, able to automatically capture and share best practices, benchmarks, and experience. Only by understanding the full context and impact of historical actions can an organization identify early indicators of success or failure, and collaborate on options by tapping the knowledge of the entire organization. Individuals make effective decisions that apply past knowledge as part of a strategic learning loop. Innovation Centers of Excellence are common to support the organization's aggressive innovation strategy.

■ **Metrics.** New metrics reflect the importance of innovation, such as revenue from new ventures, the number of ideas at various stages of the development process, the time from idea to launch, and the projected value of new ideas in the pipeline.

■ **Governance.** Innovate Level organizations have a more comprehensive and mature set of governance policies because their information management requirements are greater and more dynamic than any other level.

■ **Outsourcing.** These organizations have a strong focus on evaluating their existing line of products and services and exploring new business opportunities. This process will enable them to explore outsourcing as one of many options to restructure their current offerings, or in developing their new products and services.

■ **Change management.** Innovate Level organizations are very adaptive and willing to change course as they are driven by the innovation and the need to explore new business opportunities. This attitude creates a culture that not only expects change, but also embraces it.

People: Creative Collaborators

■ **Skills.** In addition to the people needed to run and optimize the business, the organization attracts and rewards individuals who can synthesize information and ideas from multiple industries and interpret these to propose new and viable ideas. In short, people are expected to think like entrepreneurs: Hungry ones. These people are hard to find, but the organization has made an ongoing commitment to hiring and retaining them.

- **Motivators**. This organization provides a stimulating environment for creative thinkers who like to challenge old paradigms and work outside the box. In this dynamic environment, anyone in the organization can bring a new idea to the table.

- **Dynamics**. The Innovate Level is truly a melting pot—efficiency experts mixed with creative thinkers. However, differences in background, experience, and knowledge are embraced and encouraged. Collaboration is all the richer when the participants bring unique perspectives to the table. Cross-functional peer groups continue to play a key role in an individual's day. Peer groups are always looking to broaden the diversity of the team—all the better for the most vibrant brainstorming sessions and the most creative ideas.

Culture: Entrepreneurial Innovation

- **Rewards**. Individual intuition and innovation are supported by a culture of inquiry, cooperation, and experience. The culture rewards creativity and drive and does not punish failures. Perhaps only 1 idea in 10 will be funded for further development and 1 in 100 of those actually brought to market, but that idea will be brought quickly from concept to fruition. This momentum provides a gratifying work experience for achievement-oriented teams.

- **Adaptability**. Proactive change—even "revolutionary" cultural change—is constant. There is an atmosphere of business tension in which competitive and market information constantly stimulates inventive thinking and action. The Innovate Level environment requires employees, customers, and suppliers to continuously contribute and evaluate new ideas. As with Optimize Level organizations, change is fundamental—not only accepted, but *expected*.

- **Collaboration.** Self-managed teams dominate the landscape. Collaboration is sophisticated. Diversity of experiences among these cross-functional teams leads to great originality. The culture of innovation accepts that failures are inevitable and used as learning experiences. The results of these learning experiences are documented and shared as enterprise knowledge, further developing the corporate culture.

- **Innovation.** Strategic thinking is viewed as visionary at the Optimize Level. It is expected at the Innovate Level. People think like out-of-the-box geniuses but act like team contributors with a common end goal. The organization embraces even the most outrageous new ideas, because it can accurately forecast the potential of new ideas and manage risk to within tolerable levels—while continuing to manage existing business.

- **Internal collaboration.** Innovate Level organizations are even more aggressive and dedicated to leveraging their collective talents and skills just like organizations. The difference is in the primary focus. In Innovate organizations, collective talents and skills are not only used to solve business problems, but also to explore new ideas, products, and services. These organizations strongly encourage the employees and business units to mobilize their collective talents to look for new market opportunities to launch new products and services. Key stakeholders from a variety of disciplines frequently participate in innovation Centers of Excellence to combine their collective talent to support innovation.

- **Analytical thinking.** The use of analytics is an essential core component at this level as the organization focuses on exploring new products, services, and markets. Analytics are used to understand customer needs, behaviors, and propensity to buy new products and services. External market information is integrated with internal data to provide comprehensive information to enable the application and validation of assumptions, models, and predictions. Information from partners and suppliers is also analyzed to connect the dots and produce a comprehensive analysis of potential new products and services.

■ **Social responsibility.** Innovate Level organizations are not only able to execute their strategies to address their social responsibility and sustainability, but also have the opportunity to address their social responsibility and sustainability goals in the design, development, and marketing of new products and services. Furthermore, these organizations may use their customers' awareness of social responsibility and sustainability concerns to identify new products and services.

Glossary

ad hoc
In analytics it is a query made solely in response to a specific situation or request without considering the wider or long-term repeatability issues. It is considered a reactive way to practice fact-based decision making.

adaptability
The organization's acceptance of or resistance to change.

alignment
In the context of organization maturity, it is the act of the organization to match the capabilities of the four organizational pillars (people, processes, technology, and culture) to support the organization's business priorities and objectives.

analytics
A suite of technical solutions that uses mathematical and statistical methods. The solutions are applied to data to generate insight to help organizations understand historical business performance as well as forecast and plan for future decisions.

big data
Information (both structured and unstructured) of a size and complexity that challenges or exceeds the capacity of an organization to handle, store, and analyze it.

business experts
Nontechnical users of data and information, whose input is needed to develop analytics, select key performance indicators, and use information for decision making.

business intelligence
A broad category of applications and technologies for reporting, analyzing, and providing access to data to help enterprise users make better business decisions. BI applications include the activities of decision support systems, query and reporting, and online analytical processing (OLAP).

business process
The defined method for a range of activities that organizations perform. A business process can include anything from the steps needed to make a product to how a supply is ordered or how a decision is made.

business rule
A statement of business logic that specifies conditions to be evaluated and actions to be taken if those conditions are satisfied.

business users
Non-technical individuals who use data for decision making.

Center of Excellence (CoE)
Typically a permanent, formal organizational structure consisting of representatives from both business and IT that seeks to advance and promote the proper and effective use of technology and analytics to support the organization's business strategy. Sometimes known as a Competency Center.

change agent
An organization or group of individuals tasked with introducing change in the way the organization is currently operating.

change management
The organization's effort to control and manage the introduction of new changes to the current operating model to ensure gradual and successful adoption.

cloud computing
A model for network access in which large, scalable resources are provided via the Internet as a shared service to requesting users. Access, computing, and storage services can be obtained by users without the need to understand or control the location and configuration of the system. Users consume resources as a service, and pay only for the resources that are used.

collaboration
The ability of individuals to interact effectively to support organizational goals.

cultural driver
A business leader, likely at the executive level, able to influence an organization's culture.

culture
The set of shared attitudes, values, goals, and practices that characterize a company or an organization.

customer lifetime value (CLV)
The measure of the long-term economic value of a customer. It is the sum of all the profits from a given customer over the lifetime of his or her relationship with your business.

dashboard
A view that displays ranges of data in a graphical format. Key performance indicators (KPIs) or any element can be displayed in a dashboard. Each element is represented by a gauge that displays the data ranges that are defined. Links to comments, trend data, and element properties can also be provided.

data cleansing
The process of eliminating inaccuracies, irregularities, and discrepancies from data.

data governance
The process for addressing how data enters the organization, who is accountable for it, and how that data achieves the organization's quality standards that allow for complete transparency within an organization.

data management
The process of managing data as a resource that is valuable to an organization or business, including the process of developing data architectures, developing practices and procedures for dealing with data, and then executing these aspects on a regular basis.

data mart
A subset of the data in a data warehouse. A data mart is optimized for a specific set of users who need a particular set of queries and reports.

Data Mavericks
Individuals with in-demand analytical and technical skills who have made their organization very dependent on their skills to understand data. These individuals also tend to resist efforts to broaden the use of technology in an organization as it threatens their status.

data modeling
A model that is used to either logically or physically organize the data elements in a database, including the definition of the data elements and of the relationships among the data elements for a specific industry, such as banking.

data quality
The relative value of data, which is based on the accuracy of the knowledge that can be generated using that data. High-quality data is consistent, accurate, and unambiguous, and it can be processed efficiently.

data silos
A term used to describe the process of keeping data in separate systems for use by specific business units. The information in one silo sometimes conflicts with information maintained in another silo.

data steward
An individual comfortable with both technology and business problems. Stewards are responsible for communicating between the business users and the IT community.

data value
In the context of this book, the degree to which information is valued as a corporate asset.

data visualization
The process of abstracting data in a schematic form, including attributes or variables for information units, and rendering it into visual forms such as graphs, charts, diagrams, and animations.

data warehouse
A collection of data that is extracted from one or more sources for the purpose of query, reporting, and analysis. Data warehouses are generally used for storing large amounts of data that originate in other corporate applications or that is extracted from external data sources.

decision making
How decisions are made, based on what types of resources, information, and specific processes are available.

dimension tension
A state in which the maturity level of one or more of the four organizational pillars does not match the maturity level of the other pillars.

diversity
The mix of skills, backgrounds, and knowledge that employees bring to an organization.

domain experts
Also known as subject matter experts, these individuals have an in-depth knowledge of a specific area within their business unit. The input from

domain experts is critical in making decisions about what data to use and how to use it.

dynamics
The nature of interactions among individuals within the organization and among the four organizational pillars.

enterprise resource planning (ERP)
An integrated application that controls day-to-day business operations such as inventory, sales, finance, human resources, and distribution. From the warehousing perspective, ERP systems differ from standard databases in that they have predefined data models that must be understood in order to successfully extract the data.

executive sponsor
C-level individual who sponsors enterprise and strategic changes and initiatives in an organization.

forecast
A numerical prediction of a future value for a time series. Forecasting techniques are used to identify previously unseen trends and anticipate fluctuations to facilitate better planning.

globalization
Comprehensive term for the emergence of a global society in which economic, political, environmental, and cultural events in one part of the world quickly come to have significance for people in other parts of the world.

grid computing
A type of computing in which large computing tasks are distributed among multiple computers on a network.

information access
The flow of meaningful business insight to the business users who need it.

Information Evolution Model (IEM)
The SAS organizational maturity model (patented by the U.S. government). The model provides a framework for measuring where an organization is in terms of generating and using business insight to support decisions and validate strategies.

information management process
A comprehensive step-by-step description of how information is collected, cleansed, stored, moved, and delivered to support decision making.

information value chain
A detailed layout and description of how an organization creates value and output in the form of products and services, including all the steps, input, and output required to complete this process.

infrastructure resources
The IT resources used to manage, store, and distribute enterprise information including networks, databases, application, solutions, and data warehouses.

innovation
The ability of an organization to generate and act on new or different ideas, products, or services.

intelligence tools
Applications used to transform raw data into useful knowledge.

IT architecture
The hardware, software, and connectivity that support information flow.

key performance indicator (KPI)
A measurement that shows whether an organization is progressing toward its stated goals.

master data
The data that describes the important details of a business subject area such as customer, product, or material across the organization. Master data allows different applications and lines of business to use the same definitions and data regarding the subject area. Master data gives an accurate, 360-degree view of the business subject.

master data management
The business applications, methods, and tools that implement the policies, procedures, and infrastructure to support the capture, integration, and subsequent shared use of accurate, timely, consistent, and complete master data.

maturity model
A framework that describes, for a specific area of interest, a number of levels of sophistication at which activities in this area can be carried out.

metadata
Descriptive data about data that is stored and managed in a database, in order to facilitate access to captured and archived data for further use.

metrics
The types of measures that an organization tracks to gauge its success. Also see: Key performance indicators.

motivators
The intrinsic and extrinsic forces that drive people to do what they do.

outsourcing
The transfer of the management or day-to-day execution of an entire business function to an external service provider.

performance management
The organization's effort to track, report on, and distribute its business performance information to support decision making.

rewards
The compensation structure—formal and informal—and how it shapes behavior.

scalability
The ability of a software application to function well and with minimal loss of performance, despite changing computing environments; the volume of computations, users, or data. Scalable software is able to take full advantage of increases in computing capability such as those that are provided by the use of SMP hardware and threaded processing.

service-oriented architecture (SOA)
A software design and software architecture design pattern independent of any vendor, product, or technology and based on discrete pieces of software providing application functionality as services to other applications. For instance, this software design defines how two computing entities, such as programs, interact in such a way as to enable one entity to perform a unit of work on behalf of another entity.

shared services model
A model in which an organization consolidates the offering of a service, such as analyzing data or producing business intelligence reports, in one business unit. Other units must come to that unit to get this work done.

skills
The capabilities that are sought or nurtured in the organization's knowledge worker.

social responsibility
The organization's focus on environmental, social, and humane activities.

static reports
Reports that can't be automatically updated (or refreshed) by business users.

text analytics
Refers generally to the process of deriving patterns and trends from unstructured content such as notes, reports, and comments.

transparency
Visibility in contexts related to the behavior of an organization, the manner in which it conducts business, and its relationship to customers, employees, and partners.

About the Author

Aiman Zeid heads Organizational Transformation Services for SAS Institute's Global Business Consulting unit. He has helped numerous organizations on four continents evaluate their organizational maturity and readiness to deploy business analytics. His focus on enterprise-wide approaches has made him a sought-after consultant for starting Business Analytics Centers of Excellence.

Zeid specializes in evaluating organizational maturity and readiness to deploy and use business analytics. He works with organizations in all industries to assess their technical information management infrastructure, resources and skills, processes, and culture. He has 28 years' experience in information management, business consulting, and technical implementation of business analytics and performance management solutions.

Zeid is his organization's in-house expert on SAS methodologies and is often called on to talk with analyst groups such as Forrester and Gartner. He is SAS' chief messenger for Business Analytics Centers of Excellence and helped develop the SAS Organizational Maturity Assessment methodology using the SAS Information Evolution Model. He is also a popular keynote speaker, having headlined business analytics talks in Greece, Turkey, and the Philippines. He has presented jointly with noted management consultant and author Robert Morison on "Leading an Analytical Enterprise."

Before joining Global Business Consulting, Zeid led the SAS Human Capital Management practice in North America. He holds an MBA and a BS in engineering (computer science diploma) from George Washington University. Prior to joining SAS he worked as a consultant for Battelle Institute and the Hay Group.

Index

Printed and bound by CPI Group (UK) Ltd, Croydon, CR0 4YY

16/04/2025

14658513-0001